Offshore Plundering,
by American Companies

By WALTER LAMP

OTHER BOOKS BY WALTER LAMP

99 Prescriptions for a More Ethical Society
Combating the Major Ethical Abuses of the Day:
Governance, Excessive Compensation,
Subsidies, Information Suppression
Lies and Spins, & More ISBN #9780981668116

Biblical Verses, A Frank Study of the Old Testament and Hebrew Bible
How the Scripture and the Religion Changed Over Time
What the Old Testament / Hebrew Bible Actually Says
Explaining Conflicts & Inconsistencies in the Scripture
Better Understanding All the Abrahamic Religions;
Judaism, Christianity and Islam ISBN#9780983495420

Koranic Verses, A Frank Study of the Koran
How the Koran is Honored & Dishonored in Practice
Understanding Islam's History ISBN #9780981668123

Offshore Plundering,
by American Companies

Explains the Foolish US Tax Incentives to:

- Move operations offshore
- Expand abroad rather than domestically
- Move more and more US jobs offshore
- Hoard cash offshore

Shows How to Close the Loopholes:

- Stop the US tax incentives to operate offshore
- Restore the US economic base
- Collect $ Billions in taxes owed to US Treasury
- Help balance the budget, reduce US debt
- Bring cash and jobs back home

By Walter Lamp, J.D. (Yale), CPA

®

RunningLight Publishing Company
Reno, Nevada

Offshore Plundering, by American Companies by Walter Lamp
1st Edition.

1. Income Taxes - United States 2. Taxation – International
3. Jobs 3. Ethics 4. Foreign Policy
5. Economics 6. Politics

ISBN-13: 978-0-9834954-4-4 (paperback)

Library of Congress Control Number: 2013900792

336 LAM 2013 10 9 8 7 6 5 4 3 2 1

Printed in the United States of America

Table of Contents

Introduction

The United States is being plundered abroad by its own companies, induced to do so by tax incentives the United States itself created:

- The US workforce is plundered by American companies shifting US jobs offshore.
- The US Treasury is plundered by American companies shifting taxable profits offshore.
- The US economic base is plundered by American companies shifting operation offshore.
- The US economic base is plundered by American companies expanding offshore rather than domestically.
- The US economic base is plundered by American companies maintaining huge cash hoard offshore.
- Future US generations are being plundered by inducing American companies to send American know-how and R&D offshore.
- Future US generations are being plundered by forcing budget deficits and increasing government debt.
- And much more, all resulting from a tax loophole that the United States can and should plug immediately.

Many decades ago the United States allowed the development of the "foreign subsidiary loophole" in its system of worldwide taxation that actually creates a tax incentive for American companies to conduct operation offshore and lead to what now might be called plundering. This incentive is destroying our domestic economic base, creating budgetary stalemates due to uncollected tax revenues and wreaking havoc with our ability to create jobs to employ our unemployed.

The fix is a simple change in the US tax laws; simple in nature and perhaps it will also be surprising simple to get through Congress. The fix doesn't increase taxes but rather collects already owed taxes while ending the US tax incentive to move operations offshore. In one fell swoop, (1) there would be budget-balancing collections of taxes already recorded on company books as being owed to the US Treasury, (2) tax-neutrality and an even tax playing-field would be created between domestic and offshore operations, and (3) there would be both a reining-in of US job loss and the return of some jobs that had gone offshore.

While the fix is simple, the subject matter is not that simple to explain as it concerns international or cross-border taxation, one of the more difficult areas of taxation. And the matter is made more complex by all the tax cheating and sophisticated tax gaming going on. Every effort has been made here to keep it simple so that readers, including legislators, can understand what is really going on and what is at stake.

WE HAVE A WORLDWIDE TAXATION SYSTEM. The United States taxes the worldwide income of everybody subject to US tax, individuals and companies (corporations). However, a major unintended loophole arose over the years as companies were able to use a misguided exception to the worldwide taxation system. By excluding the income of foreign subsidiaries from the US parent company's US tax return, the US parent company effectively converted, for itself, the worldwide taxation system into a territorial taxation system.

Under a territorial taxation system, only the income arising within the given territory (in this case, within the United States) would be subject to US tax. All income earned offshore would escape US taxation. The flight offshore of individuals and companies, and their assets, would be horrendous under a territorial system.

With our worldwide taxation system and the foreign subsidiary loophole to it, it is only the income of the foreign subsidiaries that escape US taxation and that was enough to wreak havoc. Thus, when a US company forms a foreign subsidiary to conduct offshore operations, worldwide taxation is avoided. Individuals cannot do this.

As an American citizen (or resident), I cannot shift my income abroad and avoid U.S. taxation. For instance, I cannot put money in a foreign bank account and exclude the interest income I earn on it from my U.S. tax return. Nor can I exclude from my U.S. tax return any income earned from my working abroad. Forming a foreign corporation and transferring my interest income or earned income (wages, fees, royalties, etc.) to that corporation would avail me nothing because the U.S. tax laws would see through this subterfuge and tax me on that income. Thus, as an individual, I am truly subject to US tax on my worldwide income under the US worldwide taxation system.

A US company is also subject to the US worldwide taxation system, except when it interposes a foreign subsidiary and runs its foreign income through that subsidiary (this is the loophole). A US company that directly earns foreign income, or conducts offshore business in its own name in a foreign branch operation, is taxed on that foreign income -- under the US worldwide taxation system, this foreign income must be included in the US company's US tax return.

Instead of conducting its offshore operation through a branch, the US company could conduct its offshore operation through a wholly-owned subsidiary incorporated in the foreign country and beat the US tax. The income of foreign subsidiary would not be included in the US parent company's US tax return and thus the income earned offshore would not be subject to US taxation. Interposing a foreign subsidiary (which is solely at the option of the US company) effectively converts the US worldwide tax system to a territorial tax system that allows offshore income to escape US tax.

The US parent company would be subject to US tax on any dividends received from its foreign subsidiary. As a result, there would be US taxation when the foreign subsidiary distributes its offshore profits to its parent company as dividends. However, this is largely theoretical because dividends are not being paid by these foreign subsidiaries.

Although it is the foreign subsidiary that would pay the dividends, whether it pays dividends is within the control of the US parent company; the company which would have to pay the US tax due on that dividend. Having the foreign subsidiary refrain from paying dividends defeats the US tax and allows the offshore profits to accumulate in the foreign subsidiary.

It has become painfully obvious that dividends are not being paid and that the accumulations of profits in the foreign subsidiaries are growing astronomically. All we have to do is look at the amount of cash being hoarded offshore in foreign subsidiaries. Two years ago it was reliably estimated that offshore cash hoards amounted to $1.4 trillion. A trillion is a thousand billion, or $1,000,000,000,000. As these offshore hoards grow year-to-year, what initially would appear to be a mere short-term deferral of the US tax turned out to be a permanent deferral with the US tax never being paid.

Allowing the sheltering of foreign operating income from US tax through use of foreign subsidiaries was an unintended loophole. It didn't look like a loophole in the unsophisticated initial days when the US tax system was created many, many decades ago. That was before the days of deliberate offshore tax sheltering when US companies were driven business needs instead of taxes.

If there were foreign opportunities for mining, oil, or manufacturing for local markets, it made sense to conduct those operations through a subsidiary created in the foreign country. Yet, even in those situations and even in that era, it was not logical to exclude the income of the foreign subsidiary from the US parent company's US tax return.

A US parent company has to include all its domestic subsidiaries in what is called its consolidated US tax return. No significant bar to the inclusion of foreign subsidiaries arises from their books of account being in local currency and their using foreign accounting methods.

Those foreign subsidiaries were included in the US parent company's consolidated Annual Report to shareholders and in SEC filings. The accountants were fully capable of properly converting the foreign currency to US dollars and converting into US accounting methods for the shareholder and SEC reports and those conversions could also be used for US tax reporting. The income of the foreign subsidiaries could have been included in the consolidated US tax returns of the US parent corporations just as that income is included in reports to shareholders and the SEC.

THE LOOPHOLE GROWS INTO OUTRIGHT PLUNDER. Why wasn't the income of foreign subsidiaries made subject to immediate US taxation like other worldwide income? Perhaps it was due to the failure to think ahead, or perhaps it was merely that exclusion didn't matter much back then.

Most of the foreign operations in the early days were unlikely to have shifted many US jobs abroad. Raw material mining had to be done locally, invariably by locals. While oil was found abroad, US oil jobs weren't being shifted to foreigners; if anything, it created offshore jobs for Americans. Manufacturing for a local market, if it concerned products too heavy to ship or produced something like electricity, was appropriately done offshore without the shifting of US jobs offshore.

In the early days, it would not have been unreasonable to believe that business reasons and not tax reasons drove the offshore operations, if, that is, any real thought was given to the matter. The US tax deferral for foreign subsidiary earnings didn't then work as an inducement to go abroad and the deferral wasn't likely to be material in amount.

The US Treasury stood only to collect US tax only to the extent the foreign tax was lower than the US tax. This matter is explained more fully in the chapter "*Avoiding Double Taxation -- The US Foreign Tax Credit System*." As the foreign operations were then business and not tax driven, operations would take place in foreign countries that had relatively high tax-rates, which left little residual tax for the US to collect. If the foreign tax rate was 30% and the US tax-rate was 35%,* the foreign subsidiary loophole would defer payment of the 5% due the US Treasury.

The amount of deferred US tax grew modestly in normal fashion over time until the US parent companies or their financial engineers realized that they could game the tax situation so as to increase the deferrals and also make the deferrals permanent; that is, never pay the tax.

Lowering the foreign taxes would increase the amount of US tax that could be deferred, and there were ways to do this. Offshore operations could deliberately be undertaken in lower tax-rate countries. Sometimes the US parent company could negotiate

---

* A flat 35% is used as the US corporate tax-rate although there is some progression in the tax-rate, particularly as to taxable income up to $75,000 which is taxed at 15% to 25%. To adjust for inflation, it makes sense to lower the corporate tax-rate on a greater amount of taxable income, say $250,000.

for a lower tax-rate or even a tax holiday if operations were to be undertaken in that country. Sometimes the financial engineers could come up with sophisticated schemes to effectively divert income from higher tax-rate countries to lower tax-rate countries. When that is done to an extreme, as where the higher tax-rate foreign country winds up collecting little or no tax, that too can be called plundering; plundering of friendly foreign governments.

OFFSHORE PLUNDERING ACCELERATED with the expansion of offshore operations funded by the profits accumulated in the foreign subsidiaries. The US tax laws had created an incentive to continue keeping the profits offshore, so domestic operations that might have been expanded gave way to offshore expansion.

Our domestic economic base was being eroded, and more and more US jobs were being lost. Digging out domestic recessions, providing US jobs for the unemployed and finding revenues to balance the national budget was becoming increasingly difficult as US parent companies shifted so much business activity offshore to take advantage of the foreign subsidiary loophole.

To the extent that the accumulated foreign profits could have possibly found use in the existing foreign operations or in expanding those operations, the accumulated profits were devoted to that use. But, eventually, there was no offshore business use for the ever accumulating profits so offshore cash balances grew and grew. The horrendous size of the existing offshore cash hoards testify to the lack of offshore uses or that cash would have already been drawn down.

As that cash is not needed in the offshore operations, it could have been remitted to the US parent companies. But why would management have their foreign subsidiaries pay dividends and trigger US taxation? There happen to be very good business reasons to bring the cash home and pay the tax, reasons that should appeal to top management. See the chapters "*Accumulated Offshore Cash*" and "*Ethical Considerations in US Foreign Policy and in Company Offshore Activities.*" Yet, the offshore cash hoards persist and the domestic economy starves.

THE DEFERRED US TAXES CAN AND SHOULD BE COLLECTED NOW. Whatever might be said to justify the initial exclusion of foreign subsidiaries from the US parent companies' US tax returns, and that would be thin at best, there is now every reason to put a stop to it. Eliminating the loophole would do more than stop the foolish US tax incentive given to US companies going offshore. It would also result in the US Treasury immediately collecting hundreds of billions of dollars of US tax that had been deferred awaiting the payment of dividends that would never be paid.

It should be noted and emphasized that the US parent companies show these deferred US taxes as outstanding liabilities in the liability section of their balance sheets in their Annual Reports to shareholders. It would have been bad shareholder accounting to report the foreign earnings as profits earned by the company and not provide for the taxes that are statutorily due in the future when those earning are paid as dividends.

As a result, generally accepted accounting requires the recognition of the deferred taxes in the accounting books as a current expense associated with earning the offshore profits then being reported to shareholders. With reported earnings have already been reduced for the deferred taxes to be paid in the future, there is no second charge to reported earnings when those deferred taxes are actually paid. Thus, contrary to the impression people are likely to have, the deferred taxes can be paid to the US Treasury without any charge to company earnings. It would be like paying any other liability reflected on the balance sheet; there is no reduction of reported earnings.

Some US parent companies are legislatively arguing for the forgiveness of their deferred taxes so that they could bring their offshore cash hoards back home without US tax and so enable them, they claim, to create domestic jobs. The last time (2005) they argued for and got a repatriation tax holiday so they could bring offshore cash home in order to provide US jobs, they brought back over $300 billion in offshore cash and devoted 92% of it to paying dividends to shareholders and buying back company stock. Two years ago the accumulated offshore cash amounted to over a trillion dollars and a similar argument is now expected.

THE UNDERLYING LEGISLATIVE POLITICS PROMISES TO BE INTERESTING. Shame on the US companies that took so much advantage of the foreign subsidiary loophole and shame on us for allowing the situation to get out of hand. But, fortunately, most US companies were not involved in the offshore plundering.

The US companies that were not involved might help politically. To be sure, the trade organizations usually dominated by the larger companies that have gone offshore would normally follow the dictates of those companies even though the trade organizations were supposed to represent all their members -- but that might not stand against a coordinated effort of the uninvolved corporations to serve their own interests.

Their own interest would be in their not having to pay the taxes the others avoided paying. Their own interest would be in re-establishing the domestic economic base, which is of less interest to those who benefit so much offshore. Their own interest would be in stemming the out-flow of US jobs and increasing the inflow, enhancing domestic purchasing power and resulting in improved markets for their products.

Some of the larger corporations that have gone offshore might agree with the elimination of the loophole -- not only for the greater good, but in their own self-interest as well. A split in the ranks is possible and would be politically significant.

Those interested in curtailing government debt and improving government revenues without increasing taxes, and those interested in not curtailing government spending for valid purposes such as education, should favor changing the law.

All in all, it is not too much to ask that the misguided policy be terminated by closing the foreign subsidiary loophole and having the US Treasury collect the taxes already owed to it.

Chapter 1

Our Worldwide System of Taxation

There are many forms of taxation in the United States.* This book deals only with income taxation on the federal level, with the focus being on international or cross-border activity where business operations are conducted in a foreign country (the "offshore" country).

Little space is devoted to the definition of "income," which presents its own difficulties. Fortunately, the accounting profession dominated by Certified Public Accountants (CPAs) has established rules defining "income" for use in preparing financial accounting reports to shareholders and to the Securities and Exchange Commission (SEC). The generally accepted accounting principles (GAAP) used in "financial accounting" are also used for

* For instance, there are customs taxes, excise taxes, inheritance taxes, payroll taxes, stamp taxes, and a host of other taxes, not to mention still more taxes on the State and local levels.

"tax accounting" purposes; that is, used for tax reporting to the US Treasury (via the Internal Revenue Service).

Both GAAP and tax accounting aim at the fair measurement of income, which is usually the same for both purposes. Where they differ, it is invariably due to special rules provided under the tax laws. For example, the tax laws provide special rules allowing faster tax deductions for depreciation aimed at providing taxpayers with a tax incentive to invest in depreciable assets rather than being aimed at the fair measurement of depreciation expense.

All types of income from all possible sources are subject to income taxation. Income includes business operating profits, wages, fees, trading gains, interest, royalties and much more.

The country in which income is earned (called "host" country) has the primary right to tax that income. The earner of that income might be based in another country (the "home" country) and it also might have the right to tax the same income.

This is where we get to the main focus of this book; the US taxation of the offshore income earned by a US business enterprise, usually a domestically incorporated entity. The US company might operate offshore in its own name (called an offshore "branch" operation) but more commonly it incorporates a local subsidiary to conduct its offshore operations (usually an Irish corporation in Ireland, a Chinese corporation in China and so forth). In such a structure, the US business enterprise is called the US parent company and its foreign subsidiary conducts the offshore operation.

UNDER THE US WORLDWIDE TAX SYSTEM, the United States taxes the worldwide income of everybody subject to US tax, individuals and companies (corporations).

As the United States provides a credit for foreign taxes paid on foreign income (covered in the chapter, "*Avoiding Double*

Taxation -- The US Foreign Tax Credit System"), the worldwide tax system is designed to create a form of tax-neutrality between domestic and offshore operations. Overall, Americans would wind up paying the US rate of tax whether income is earned offshore or in the United States, with the exception that the taxpayer would be saddled with additional tax to the extent the foreign tax-rate is higher than the US tax-rate.

The worldwide taxation system was designed so that Americans, individuals and companies, would not pay a lower rate of tax on income earned offshore than they would pay on income earned domestically. By aiming at presenting Americans with no US tax incentive to either operate abroad or in the United States, the worldwide tax system would have allowed business considerations, rather than tax considerations to drive business decisions.

The worldwide tax system served the United States well until a misguided exception for foreign subsidiaries developed into a major loophole, creating a US tax incentive for US parent companies to move business operations offshore to lower tax-rate countries.

A territorial tax system would provide a very broad incentive to both individuals and businesses to move income producing activities offshore to lower tax-rate countries. A territorial tax system would have the United States tax only the income earned within its borders and thus deliberately allow the wholesale avoidance of US tax by both individual and companies. For instance, the finances of an American individual could be structured in such a way (like using foreign bank accounts) as to escape US tax because the income would be earned outside the United Sates. The foreign bank would be selected based on it being located in a country that does not tax that type of income or does not tax at all (generally called a "tax-haven"). Thus, a US territorial tax system would be a bonanza for tax-havens.

Under a US territorial tax system, an American company could chose to supply its US customers from an offshore plant and thus pay no US tax. If the plant were located in a country that doesn't tax, or provides negotiated tax holidays, all income taxation would be avoided.

Thus, under a territorial tax system, the United States would face the specter of American individuals relocating their assets to rocks in the middle of the ocean (rocks that do not happen to tax) and American companies relocating plants offshore in low tax countries or countries providing tax breaks. The United States understandably rejected the territorial tax system and adopted the worldwide taxation system.

Fortunately, the US worldwide taxation system functions as it should function with respect to American individuals. It is a relatively tight system that forces the tax cheats to commit criminal acts as they try to beat the system.

Unfortunately, the United States makes it easy for US companies to beat the US worldwide taxing system legally. Unbelievably, the United States provided a distinct US tax incentive for them to do so. American companies, but not American individuals, can form and own a foreign subsidiary to conduct offshore operations and avoid US tax. And they have done so, relocating US plants offshore through this "foreign subsidiary loophole."

THE FOREIGN SUBSIDIARY LOOPHOLE effectively converts the US worldwide tax system to a territorial tax system with respect to the earning of those offshore subsidiaries.

All domestically incorporated subsidiaries of a US parent company must be included in parent company's US tax return on Form 1120, basically taxing the parent on the earnings of the entire consolidated group. However, in what has become the loophole of concern here, the United States requires the US parent company to exclude its foreign incorporated subsidiaries from the consolidated tax return. Thus, the offshore income earned by the foreign subsidiaries is not subject to US tax.

If and when a foreign subsidiary pays its offshore earning out as a dividend to its US parent company, the receipt of the dividend is treated as US parent company income subject to US tax. But the hard facts show that the foreign subsidiaries do not pay their earnings out as dividends; they hoard those earnings offshore, accumulating huge offshore cash balances now estimated in the trillions of dollars.

Proponents of the foreign subsidiary loophole would argue that the worldwide taxation system is followed and fulfilled in that there is taxation of the offshore earning when the foreign subsidiaries pay dividends, but it would just be lip service. The ever increasing huge offshore cash hoards prove, as a factual matter, that offshore earning are just not paid out as dividends. The avoidance of US tax through the foreign subsidiary loophole has effectively becomes permanent.

THERE IS NO JUSTIFICATION for the foreign subsidiary loophole to the US worldwide taxation system. Decades ago when the worldwide taxation system was established, things were simple. Offshore operations were in the embryo stage and the full ramifications of not immediately taxing US parent companies on the current earnings of their foreign subsidiaries were not appreciated.

The exclusion of foreign subsidiaries from the consolidated US tax returns of their US parent companies did not initially represented the tax loophole that it became over time. The exclusion came into law in a much simpler age when business responded to economic needs and went abroad when it made business sense.

Some industries must conduct their type of business in foreign countries, as is the case in mining, oil exploration, producing electricity and the like. Manufacturing for a local market by locating a plant there would make sense when the market became large enough to economically justify it instead of serving it on an export basis from the US mainland.

But even under these circumstances, there was no reason to exclude the foreign subsidiary from the US parent company's US tax return. In the parallel situation of financial reporting, foreign subsidiaries are included in the Annual Reports to shareowners and the SEC.

The required information for inclusion is available even though foreign subsidiaries keep their books in local currency and use foreign accounting principles. Conversions to US dollars and to US generally accepted accounting principles (GAAP) already takes place for financial reporting purposes and would also serve for tax reporting purposes. With the necessary information thus being available for tax reporting purposes, there was never much of an information excuse for excluding foreign subsidiaries from the US parent company's US tax return, and certainly no excuse in this computer age.

Perhaps the exclusion was initially allowed for simplicity purposes. Exclusion would simplify the preparation of the US parent company's tax return, but such an argument would have also applied to excluding foreign subsidiaries from the financial accounting reports. Of course, the simplicity argument would not be advanced for financial accounting purposes because of the desire to report more and more profits to shareholders, but serves to report and less and less profits for tax accounting purposes.

Besides, GAAP accounting would not allow the exclusion of offshore operations for financial reporting purposes because it would not be a fair presentation of the enterprises activities. Yet, somehow, the exclusion of foreign subsidiaries for tax reporting purposes was felt justifiable.

Perhaps the exclusion was merely based on there initially not being enough potential US tax collections to bother with the matter. Today, with trillions of dollars of cash accumulated offshore in foreign subsidiaries, there must be hundreds of billions of dollars of US tax not yet collected as estimated in the chapter "*Accumulated Offshore Cash*."

Whatever the initial reason for excluding foreign subsidiaries from the US parent companies' US tax returns (whether it be simplicity, immateriality, miscalculation or merely un-intended and un-anticipated consequences), it has by this time become painfully clear that the exclusion operates as a loophole that should be plugged.

AMERICAN CITIZENS ARE SUBJECT TO THE US WORLDWIDE TAXATION SYSTEM. They are taxed on all their income, wherever earned. They do not have any major loophole like US parent companies have in the foreign subsidiary loophole. They cannot open interest bearing deposit accounts in foreign banks and avoid paying US tax on the interest earned.

Nor could American individual avoid US tax by forming a foreign corporation to funnel such deposits offshore because the United States would effectively disregard the subterfuge and tax them on the interest earned. The same thing would happen if they attempted to funnel their offshore wages, fees, royalties and such through such a foreign corporation.

Thus, in a sense, the US worldwide taxing system is tighter when it comes to the taxation of individual Americans. Some Americans manage to save some US tax though sophisticated financial planning abroad, and many try to hide their foreign income by resorting to what might be criminal activity to evade US taxes. US individuals do have not an easy path to US tax avoidance as US parent companies have in the foreign subsidiary loophole.

Americans living abroad complain about the new form they have to file with the IRS reporting detailed information on their offshore bank and other financial accounts and the income earned thereon.* The IRS has even been accused of shifting the cost of compliance to the private sector, ostensibly because the IRS should be able to catch the tax cheats without burdening legitimate taxpayers with additional filing requirements. No mention is made of the enormous burden placed on the IRS by the vast amount of tax cheating taking place and no mention is made of the limited staff the IRS has because of budgetary constraints. Also, no mentions is made that other taxpayers, you and me, have to make up the revenue shortfall created by the tax cheats so we should be in favor of the IRS getting the funding it needs to enforce our laws.

Going still further, the anti-tax forces argue that the United States should stop taxing citizens residing abroad with their only reason being that many other countries, but not all, exempt their non-resident citizens from tax. This, of course, would get rid of the compliance forms, somewhat similar to throwing out the baby with the bathwater. Just free the non-resident US citizens from US taxation and no tax reporting at all would be required. That no tax would be collected goes unmentioned, to say nothing of having to increase the taxes of others (you and me).

What is essentially being argued is that we should depart from our worldwide taxation system and adopt a territorial tax system, which would create a substantial tax incentive for many Americans to move abroad and further depress US tax revenues. Unlike the big loophole US parent companies have to avoid US tax by going abroad, individuals have no such loophole. That is why individuals resort to outright criminal tax cheating and the IRS has such a huge compliance problem.

---

* "*For Americans Abroad, Taxes Just Got More Complicated,*" by David Jolly, The New York Times, April 15, 2012.

The compliance problem has existed for decades. Back in 1983 a Senate study found that the use of offshore banks had become pervasive, it having grown four-fold to $230 billion between 1975 and 1981.[*] In 2001, Americans were believed to have more than $800 billion on deposit in just a single tax-haven, the Cayman Islands, and it was estimated that $70 billion in tax was evaded annually.[†] By 2011, some 20,000 Americans came forward under two voluntary disclosure programs that allowed them avoid criminal penalties on their tax cheating, 20,000 being just a fraction of the suspected number of tax evaders,[‡] and the civil fines were steep.[§] Obviously, the compliance problem was and is enormous but some still pound on the IRS. So far, score it for the tax cheats and their financial engineers.[**]

Under territorial taxation system, individuals would be able to move offshore and avoid US tax. Hollywood can move to a tax-haven and the players become non-residents of the United States free of US and probably also free of foreign tax. We can watch professional sporting events played abroad instead of in the United States so as to enable the millionaire ball players to become non-residents free of US tax.

What the advocates of territoriality are suggesting would basically deplete US tax revenues and shift the tax burden of maintaining our society to poor souls (you and me) who don't earn enough to justify becoming non-residents for tax purposes. Of course, a non-resident can spend a fair amount of time in the

---

[*] "*Offshore Banking Perils Cited in a Senate Study*," by Jeff Gerth, The New York Times, March 15, 1983.

[†] "*Tax Enforcer Says Cheating Is on the Rise*," by David Cay Johnston, The New York Times, July 19, 2001.

[‡] "*U.S. Target Clients Directly in Hunt for Cash Hidden Offshore*," by Reuters, The New York Times, December 29, 2011.

[§] "*Voluntarily Disclose Your Offshore Accounts or Else*," by Paul Sullivan, The New York Times, August 26, 2011.

[**] "*These Islands Aren't Just a Shelter From Taxes*," by Robert M. Morgenthau, The New York Times, May 5, 2012. Also "*These Islands Aren't Just a Shelter From Taxes*," by David Cay Johnson, The New York Times, May 5, 2012.

United States but would have to pay tax to the extent he or she works here. Obviously, most of the work would take place offshore.

Sadly to say, we are approaching something like that in certain industries. Robert M. Morgenthau, former US District Attorney in Manhattan,* said that Luxemburg looks like the real capital of the music industry as so much music sales have been diverted through it. This can be done today through financially engineering the sale of the products and/or the transfer of intangible rights offshore. But the United States still has the musicians.

With a territorial taxation system, tiny Luxemburg wouldn't be able to house all the American musicians who would relocate. To be sure, some concerts will still take place in the United States. Of course, the United States shouldn't adopt any type of territorial taxation system. A possible solution to part of the compliance problem is being offered in the chapter "*Combating Offshore Plundering -- Other Suggested Legislative Changes.*"

* "*These Islands Aren't Just a Shelter From Taxes*," by Robert M. Morgenthau, The New York Times, May 5, 2012.

Chapter 2

Accumulated Offshore Cash

The accumulated offshore cash referred to here is the cash owned by and appearing on the balance sheet of a foreign subsidiary which, in turn, is owed by a US parent company. By virtue of ownership, the US parent company would include ("consolidate") its foreign subsidiaries in the accounting reports to its shareholder and in SEC filings. As a result, the accumulated cash of the foreign subsidiary also appears as cash on the consolidated balance sheet of the US parent company, although that cash actually belongs to the foreign subsidiary and is on its books of account.

Leaving out special circumstances, the cash accumulated over time on the foreign subsidiary's books came from the profits earned by the foreign subsidiary. It is what remains of the foreign subsidiary's profit after the payment of foreign tax. Part of the cash might have been invested by the foreign subsidiary in expanding its operations, so the cash accumulated at any point in time is the cash that then remains in the coffers of the foreign subsidiary. That cash is necessarily held offshore and it includes "cash equivalent" temporary investments readily convertible into cash.

The accumulated offshore cash held by foreign subsidiaries of US parent companies has grown into trillions of dollars due to the reluctance of the US parents companies to have their foreign subsidiaries pay-up their accumulated cash as dividends to the US parent companies. Repatriation the cash "home" to the United States as dividends would trigger the payment of the deferred US tax on the foreign earnings.

As previously explained, the foreign subsidiary loophole to the US worldwide system of taxation delays the actual payment of US tax on the earning of foreign subsidies to the time those earning as paid-up to the US parents as dividends. Technically, it is the receipt of the dividend that subjects the US parent company to tax on the foreign earnings. The accountants however record the deferred US tax when the US parent company consolidates the earning of their foreign subsidiaries for financial reporting purposes.

Just as the foreign subsidiary loophole makes it advantageous to retain the foreign earnings offshore, it is also advantageous to reinvest that cash in expanding foreign operations. With reinvestment, the old tax benefit is preserved and still more profits will accumulate offshore that will also benefit from the foreign subsidiary loophole.

The incentive is to reinvest offshore as much of the accumulated cash as is possible, leading to the suggestion that what remains in the foreign coffers essentially cannot find an offshore use. Yet, the offshore cash remains offshore instead of being repatriated home to the United States for use domestically. And the question arises whether the advantage of postponing the payment of the already recorded deferred taxes is worthwhile?

While the wisdom of accumulating cash offshore might well be challenged, corporate Treasurers would seem to advocate it. They are earning money on those accumulations, their profit centers and bonuses are flourishing, and they have a handy justification for keeping the funds offshore; tax would have to be paid to the US Treasury if the funds were dividended to the US parent company.

Top management might not be aware of all the ramifications of continuing to retain the cash offshore and the advantages of voluntarily repatriating the cash back to the United States and paying the deferred taxes.

MOST OF THE CASH would remain with the US parent company when the offshore cash is repatriated. Only a lesser part of the cash accumulated offshore would go to pay the US tax due, not the entire amount as some might think or were led to believe. Even when the lowest-taxed foreign income is paid-up as dividends, the bulk of the cash will remain in the coffers of the US parent company.

At the extreme, where absolutely no foreign tax had been paid on the offshore earning, the US parent company would get to keep 65% of the cash repatriated.* And this is the worst-case scenario in terms of how much of the cash offshore accumulation would remain with the US parent company. The US parent company gets to keep a greater proportion of the offshore accumulated cash if foreign tax had been paid by the foreign subsidiary.

---

* To illustrate, the foreign subsidiary earns $100 and pays no foreign tax, the $100 being represented by cash shown on the asset side of the foreign subsidiary's balance sheet. That accumulated cash is paid-up as a dividend to the US parent company. Upon receipt of the $100 dividend, the US parent company has to pay $35 (100 x 0.35 = 35) in tax to the US Treasury and retains $65, or 65%.

This should be obvious when you consider that the US parent company gets to keep 100% of the cash repatriated from foreign subsidiaries subject to high foreign tax-rates. The chapter "*Avoiding Double Taxation -- The US Foreign Tax Credit System*" explains how the United States gives a credit for the foreign taxes paid, which, if equal to or higher than the US tax-rate of 35%, results in the US parent company paying no US tax on the dividends received. Because of this, the practice arose of foreign subsidiaries subject to low foreign taxes accumulating their earnings abroad while the foreign subsidiaries subject to high foreign taxes paid-up their earnings as dividends.

Thus, the US parent company stands to keep between 100% and 65% (worst case) of the repatriated offshore cash. This is a far cry from the erroneous belief that all the money will go to pay US tax if the offshore cash is repatriated, which seems to be the prevailing belief.

- 100% of the cash repatriated would be retained by the US parent company if the foreign tax-rate were 35% or higher.
- 87% of the cash repatriated would be retained if the foreign tax-rate were 25%.*
- 72% retained if the foreign tax-rate were 10%.
- 65% retained if no foreign tax were paid, the worst case scenario.

It is believed that the existing offshore cash accumulations had been subject to a foreign tax load roughly averaging to 10%. High-taxed foreign earnings that survived the tax-reduction efforts being conducted by US parent companies were probably distributed as dividends. As a result, the accumulated offshore cash would represent foreign earning subject to lower foreign tax-

---

* The computation is somewhat complex. $100 of pre-tax earnings, less $25 foreign tax paid, leaves $75 of after- tax earnings available for the payment of a dividend. Of the $75 dividend received, $10 would go to pay the US tax ($35 US tax less a foreign tax credit of $25 equals $10). Thus, $65 of the cash received would be retained. That is 87% of the cash received (75 x 0.87 = 65).

rates, with perhaps a significant part having borne little or no foreign tax due to tax-reduction efforts. This would indicate that about 72% of the presently existing offshore cash accumulations would remain in the coffers of the US parent companies if they repatriated all the offshore cash.

THE OFFSHORE CASH ACCUMULATIONS ARE HUGE. It is estimated to be in the trillions of dollars. A trillion dollars staggers the imagination; $1,000,000,000,000. A trillion is 1,000 billion, and a billion dollars ($1,000,000,000) is enough to stagger the imagination of those of us who aren't even millionaires ($1,000,000).

A reliable estimate made in 2011 had the offshore cash at $1.375 trillion.[*] A single US parent company was known to have $74 billion in offshore cash[†] or perhaps $100 billion.[‡]

The accumulated offshore cash is what remains after as much cash as possible was probably used to fund offshore expansion. The United States creating a US tax incentive to move operations abroad is troublesome enough without considering that the United States concomitantly created an incentive to use the offshore profits to expand offshore rather than repatriate those profits to fund domestic expansion.

As the purpose in accumulating cash offshore is to put-off or avoid the payment of US tax, using the offshore cash to expand offshore operations or pursue new offshore opportunities would be very appealing if not imperative. This suggests that, at any point in time, as much cash as possible was already used in reinvesting

---

* "*In Autonomy Deal, A Way for H.P. to Spend Overseas Cash*," Michael J. De La Merced, The New York Times, August 18, 2011.

† "*How Apple Sidesteps Billions in Taxes*," by Charles Duhigg and David Kocieniewski, The New York Times, April 28, 2012.

‡ "*Overseas Cash and the Tax Games Multinationals Play*," by Victor Fleischer, The New York Times, October 3, 2012.

offshore. Thus, the size of the remaining offshore cash hoard would signal the extent to which the company is motivated by tax reduction. Huge offshore cash accumulations on the balance sheet signal that management is driven by averting taxes. When offshore cash accumulations get to be so very large, it becomes obvious that no offshore business use for those funds remains untapped and that the cash is just not needed offshore. And yet, the aversion to repatriation remains.

REPATRIATING OFFSHORE FUNDS makes perfect sense if there are any domestic uses for the money. Repatriation would also avoid some inherent foreign risks, which are discussed separately below. Within the context of there being no business purpose (as contrasted to a tax purpose) in keeping the funds offshore, the possible domestic uses take on more meaning.

A very telling case for bringing the money home can be made when repatriation is put in the context of offshore uses being exhausted and considering that:

- domestic uses for funds always exist.
- expropriation and other foreign country risk would be avoided.
- there will be no charge to earnings in repatriating the offshore cash.
- a relatively small proportion of the repatriated cash goes to pay the deferred US taxes.
- little is actually saved by deferring the US tax.
- much unnecessary expense can be eliminated by collapsing the elaborate offices and intercompany procedures needed to game foreign taxes.
- potential customer backlash throughout the world is avoided by gaining stature as a good corporate citizen.

THE DOMESTIC USES FOR FUNDS is not only to be found in connection with modernizing or expanding existing operations. Acquisitions can complement existing business activities or allow the company to strike off on new paths. There are many, many domestic uses for the offshore funds.

It is most difficult to believe that new opportunities are not to be found in America. The products being manufactured offshore were invented here. And Americans haven't stopped innovating. So why aren't domestic uses for offshore funds being found? A subtle reason lurks here, one that would not meet the eye.

The foreign subsidiary loophole induces management to ignore pursuing opportunities domestically when they could be pursued offshore and achieve a tax advantage. The subtle reason is that management of this mindset does not want to find domestic uses for the offshore funds. Domestic use would involve domestic investment and they would rather invest offshore and save tax. Management is thus blind-sighted to the domestic opportunities that have to exist, that have always existed; or being faced with a good opportunity, they just pursue it abroad.

This is why US parent companies would not provide US jobs as they promised to do so when they were pursuing a temporary US tax holiday for repatriating offshore cash. They couldn't provide US jobs without expanding domestic business operations and they preferred to expand abroad.

US parent companies got a repatriation tax holiday back in 2005 based on their promise to create US jobs with the money repatriated; US jobs that didn't materialize. The US parent companies actually repatriated $312 <u>billion</u> of offshore cash, 92% of which was shown by a reliable independent organization to have been used to pay dividends to shareholders and buy-back stock.*

---

* "*Companies Push for Tax Break on Foreign Cash*," by David Kocieniewski, The New York Times, June19, 2011.

This is not to say that using funds to pay dividends to shareholders or buy-back company stock is not a good use for the money or does not represent a valid financial purpose. The actual use of close to $300 billion of repatriated tax holiday cash for shareholder dividends and stock buy-backs show these uses to be valid domestic uses; uses that should be added to the list of possible domestic uses for the cash accumulating offshore.

Putting American innovation to work in America by manufacturing the new products domestically assumes that the US parent companies still have the production capacity to manufacture products domestically. The issue surfaces because so much has been shifted offshore that one wonders about what remains. So there is still another domestic business use for the offshore funds, perhaps the most important one: the rebuilding of domestic production capacity.

Of course, repatriated offshore cash could be used by the US parent company to pay off domestic borrowings if there are any. Having cash on one side of the consolidated balance sheet and borrowings on the other side blows-up the balance sheet, would normally be to a company's disadvantage. However in the Alice in Wonderland world of financial engineer this could present an advantage if the offshore cash produces tax-free income offshore while the offsetting domestic borrowings produce domestic tax deductions for the interest paid. Nevertheless, the existence of domestic borrowings would show that there is still another domestic use for offshore funds, and this would be still another reason for closing the foreign subsidiary loophole.

EXPROPRIATION, CHANGE IN LAW, AND OTHER RISKS lurk behind the offshore cash accumulations.

Also, if the offshore cash is retained in the local foreign currency or converted to other foreign currencies to enhance yields, exchange risks are being taken. Only too frequently we see

US parent companies announcing that earnings were negatively impacted by adverse foreign exchange fluctuations. However, the offshore cash can usually be converted from foreign currency to US dollars and placed in US dollar investments so to avoid the exchange risk.

Corporate treasurers could avoid the currency exchange risk by having the offshore funds kept in US dollars. However, where higher yields can be obtained in foreign currencies, they might be tempted to be in those currencies instead of US dollars. Such higher yields do impact profit-center results, and incentive compensation and earnings reported to shareholders. The same might be said with respect to credit risks domestically and offshore. These risks are essentially known because they are reflected in the yield. The higher the yield, the greater the risk being taken. The premium being earned when additional risk is being taken measures that risk.

The accounting profession hasn't gotten to the point of requiring that a reserve be set up for the foreign country risk being taken (similar to a reserve for bad debts). So the US parent company earnings and profit-centers look good when such higher yielding foreign assets are held in foreign subsidiaries, until something happens.

We see this today in investments denominated in Greek currency and also in investments denominated in some other currencies. Just look at the yields being obtained today for taking such risk. And the premium yield being earned for taking the risk is reported as current profit, which is great until something happens and then it is disaster. It's like a ticking bomb.

Many decades ago, it was the less developed country debt, and, much more recently, it was the subprime mortgage-backed securities that provided premium yields and attracted increasing allocations of capital or permission to so invest more and more -- until the paid-for risk materialized and disaster struck. And as to these, the most sophisticated investors, the very best professionals at the very best and biggest commercial banks got stuck.

The point in mentioning all of this is to suggest that this is an area that industrial companies should not be involved in. They are not in the business of accumulating, maintaining and managing huge amounts of cash. They don't have the expertise, nor can they really buy it. Nor should they want to oversee it. It is just not their business, yet they are forced into it by pursuing tax reduction that probably isn't worth the effort.

And then there is the risk of outright expropriation or of a change in law that would bar repatriation of the accumulated cash. These risks might be considered minimal at the present time, but there is no telling what might happen in the future. Should there be an alert, or even a mere hint of waning relationships with local politicians or on the inter-government level, there might not be time to run for the exits, especially if others are running for the exits at the same time.

It is one thing to conduct business offshore and accept these risks. They are inherent in offshore operations. It is an entirely different thing to voluntarily expose additional assets to these risks, which is what the offshore cash accumulations do; in abundance.

Some US parent companies might be voluntarily exposing billions of dollars in their foreign subsidiaries to expropriation, remittance, change-in-law and other risks, while earning precious little if anything in doing so. Also, there are many other drawbacks in hoarding cash offshore that can be considered harmful without even considering these risks.

Why corporate management should want to take such risks is one aspect? On another level the question might be asked as to why Congress and the Administration would provide a US tax incentive for US parent companies to do so by perpetuating the foreign subsidiary loophole that is the driving force behind it? Furthermore, there are foreign policy aspects to this. Where is the national interest? What might we be induced or forced to do to protect assets voluntarily kept abroad in order to save tax?

But, getting back to the company level, why are the offshore cash accumulations being perpetuated by management? Perhaps management is not convinced that they should voluntarily repatriate. Perhaps it is inertia. Perhaps it is a macho desire to stick to a course no matter what. Perhaps it's the hope of getting another repatriation tax holiday so that the cash can be brought home without US tax (and with reporting a large windfall profit).

The latter is unrealistic, not probable or even possible. The probably is that the foreign subsidiary loophole will be closed and the deferred tax required to be paid. If so, it would be a convenient exit, one to be favored and not opposed.

The appropriate time to reconsider and repatriate the offshore cash seems to be now. Interest rates are low so the value of the interest-free loan from the US Treasury is at a low point. Expropriation risk seems to be low, and there are currently no bars to remitting funds. Also, the media and the public seem to be getting particularly active in criticizing corporate management, which is likely to continue if not expand if management sticks to the beaten path. The ethical and good corporate citizen aspects are looming larger.

SURPRISINGLY, REPORTED EARNINGS WILL NOT BE CHARGED should the foreign subsidiaries pay up their accumulated cash as dividends. Here we are dealing with the interplay between financial and tax accounting, a complex matter for non-accountants more fully explained in the chapter "*Shareholder Accounting for Offshore Operations (GAAP).*"

Simply stated, upon repatriation the US tax would have to be paid, but that tax had already been provided for in the shareholder financial statements, previously reducing reported earnings. There is no further reduction in earnings when that tax is actually paid upon repatriation of the offshore cash.

This may come as a surprise as not paying tax is usually the name of the game. But here, the actual payment does not impact reported earnings. Reported earnings were already impacted because of the accounting rule that forces all expenses relating to the current period, even though payable later, to be accounted for currently. Thus, it is not the payment of the tax that is crucial. The offshore cash can be repatriated and the deferred tax paid without a charge to earnings.

Payment of the deferred tax does terminate the interest-free loan the US Treasury effectively gave the company when it allowed the company to defer payment of the tax owed. Those funds could be and probably are invested earning interest. With interest rates being very low nowadays, little is being earned.

It is not possible to tell what is being earned on the funds supplied interest-free by the US Treasury. In order to protect the foreign earnings from being taxed in the United States, those earnings must be kept offshore. You will recall that repatriation forces payment of the US tax which can amount to no more than 35% of the amount distributed, the other 65% remaining in company coffers. Thus, delaying the payment of the 35% necessitates keeping the 65% offshore as well.

Comparing the earning potential of the offshore cash while it is being retained offshore to the earning potential of the cash remaining after repatriation gets complicated. Investing 100% of the accumulated cash offshore has to be compared to investing 65% (or more) in the United States. The gamut of available and permissible investments offshore and at home differs, as does the various risks being taken offshore and at home. This makes a reliable independent comparison impossible without having actual numbers and they haven't been published.

Making-up numbers that wouldn't even qualify as a rough estimates, but just trying to sensitize the matter, it seems that there is a reported earnings stand-off in investing 100% of the cash offshore as compared to investing 65% of the cash in the United States.* Not knowing what the relative interest yields are, it was assumed the US yield was double the foreign yield so as to reflect the greater variety of possible investments and the better risk-adjusted profiles at home.

Obviously those numbers can and should be challenged. Nevertheless, it does seem that the value of the interest-free loan from the US Treasury is not significant. Not enough to justify enduring all the problems the offshore accumulation presents. Probably not even enough to cover all the added expenses that are being incurred in order to reduce foreign taxes.

An excellent case can be made for management voluntarily repatriating the offshore cash and getting off the treadmill. And a separate case can be made for Congress effectively forcing it by repealing the foreign subsidiary loophole.

CUSTOMER BACKLASH against perceived tax avoidance by US parent companies could become a growing problem. The core company business could be negatively impacted by adverse public relations arising from tax-reduction efforts in the United States or offshore.

Occupy Wall Street type protests against what the protesters would say is social injustice hasn't morphed into specific product protests or protests directed at a specific company. However, in the United Kingdom, a protest against a company's core business stores has been threatened because of what appeared

---

* Assume there is $100 in offshore cash and that investing 65% of that in the United States upon repatriation could earn say 6% or $3.90 ($65 x 0.06 = $3.90), which would leave 2.43% ($3.90 – 0.35(%) = $2.43) after US tax. Compare that to say 3% earned offshore on 100% of the funds invested offshore or $3.00 ($100 x 0.03 = $3.00) free of foreign tax; 1.95% or $1.95 ($3.00 – 0.35(%) = $1.95) after providing for the deferred US tax. The relatively small difference between 2.43% and 1.95% is largely a stand-off.

to the potential protestors to be tax-reduction efforts of the company.*

Tax-reduction efforts are sometimes undertaken by US parent companies to increase the benefit obtained through the US foreign subsidiary loophole. The lower the foreign taxes incurred, the greater the US tax deferral and the larger the offshore cash accumulation.†

Although it is not always visible, important company constituencies might be harboring some negative thoughts because of extent to which a company avoids taxes. Some US companies pay little or no US tax and that doesn't sit well with the American public. Media attention is great and ever increasing as reporters and reporting become more sophisticated in tax matters, as witness the articles cited in this book. We've also seen public attention directed at taxes paid in our recent election, and a foreign counterpart appears to be surfacing in the form of a threatened public protest.

The general public as a company constituency might be a little broad, but a company not being viewed favorably by the general public still might hurt. Customers, shareholders and investor constituencies are more directly involved. Some customer sales might be lost, or customer mindset changed so as to welcome future replacement products made by competitors. Shareholders might not like what is going on, and the media attention given to it,

---

* "*Starbucks Offers to Pay More British Tax Than Required*," by Eric Pfanner, The New York Times, December 6, 2012.

† The tax-reduction efforts are aimed directly at reducing specific foreign country taxes where a foreign subsidiary of the US parent company is conducting business. The tax reduction procedure usually entails payments that increase the offshore cash accumulation in an affiliated foreign subsidiary. The taxes avoided don't go to increase the bottom-line of the earnings statement the accountants prepare for shareholders because they have to charge earnings for the deferred tax due the US Treasury.

By reducing foreign taxes, greater advantage is being taken of the US foreign subsidiary loophole. The advantage is a timing advantage. The US tax is delayed while the foreign tax was reduced currently.

and quietly sell their stock. Sophisticated professional investors might be discounting the quality of earnings and depressing the value of the company stock. None of this will bode well for a US parent company.

Management should also be concerned, like politicians recently found out, that tax reduction can go too far. Compatriots, board members and others might silently look askance at the presumed leaders of our society fostering, harboring or perpetuating the suspect tax reduction practices being criticized in the press or the little amount of tax their company pays. Getting the monkeys off managements' backs by reversing course chould be attractive.

Digging in their heels by emphasizing the company's right to reduce its taxes (and pointing to different kinds of taxes still being paid) no longer works to assuage public criticism. The better and more honorable course appears to be reversing course and building up the company's reputation as being a good corporate citizen worldwide, a matter addressed in the chapter "*Ethical Considerations in US Foreign Policy and in Company Offshore Activities*."

Consumer backlashes, should they arise, would be a significant problem for top management. Management would be well advised to address the matter before it picks up steam, before public picketing actually arises and before it potentially turns into public boycotts.

On balance, pursing the foreign subsidiary loophole does not seem worthwhile and would not be worth wasting effort to keep it from being closed. Going much further by repatriating offshore cash, unwinding extreme tax-reduction strategies and publically endorsing the foreign subsidiary loophole closing would lead to wondrous public applause.

Chapter 3

Moving US Jobs Offshore

The process of moving US jobs offshore might have started with importing a small part of the company product line that wasn't worth manufacturing domestically or that could be manufactured cheaply offshore due to lower wage rates. That led to component manufacturing offshore, to contract manufacturing of whole products offshore and then to the shifting of domestic manufacturing plants to offshore locations. Along the way foreign subsidiaries were formed to conduct the offshore operations. This allowed the US parent companies to benefit from the foreign subsidiary loophole and accelerated the process of moving production and operations abroad, resulting in the loss of more and more US jobs.

The loss of US jobs could no longer be rationalized as solely the function of wage differentials as it has been in the distant past. In significant part, the loss of US jobs in recent decades can be attributed to the foreign subsidiary loophole. Plug the loophole and the tax motivated loss of US jobs would stop. And loophole closing is likely to start returning some jobs to the United States.

THE EROSION OF THE US JOB BASE has had and continues to have severe domestic impact in a number of respects. The personal toll on the newly unemployed and their families has been horrendous. Their loss of purchasing power impacted the domestic marketplace for goods and services. Domestic wage rates stagnated, also reducing purchasing power further slowing domestic economic growth.

Decades ago it was suggested that the shifting of US jobs offshore freed up our well-educated and well-trained workers for higher-level jobs that would make better use of their advanced skills. Let foreign workers make sneakers while American workers made computers. Today, foreign workers make both sneakers and computers. We might have lost much of our capacity to manufacture the new high-tech products.

The United States should obviously strive to reverse the situation. Terminating the foreign subsidiary loophole would be a major step in that direction. It would curtail the outflow of still more jobs and also set the stage for the return of some jobs.

OUTSOURCING BACK OFFICE SERVICES is very different from transferring manufacturing offshore or even from outsourcing computer programming. To be sure, outsourcing back office services results in the loss of US jobs just like offshore-manufacturing or computer programming would do. The differences arise in terms of the long-term negative effect on the US economic base.

Offshore call-centers, processing payrolls and claims abroad, and the other offshore back-office activities provide savings due to lower offshore wages.* Some of these activities present difficulties due to cultural differences, but still more US customers use them over time. Frequently these operations are conducted by independent companies owned and managed by foreign entrepreneurs and the US company just contracts for their services.

The adverse impact on the US economic base is much greater when it comes to shifting manufacturing offshore, or conducting scientific research, computer programming and other technical services offshore. In addition to the loss of US jobs, those activities transfer know-how offshore and enhance foreign skills that can result in more US job loss over time. This is addressed in the next chapter "*Moving Research & Know-How Offshore*."

It has been said that the loss of US jobs will reverse itself as foreign wage-rates increase due to local economic growth. Experience has shown that increasing wage rates in one foreign country only too frequently results in the transfer of the business to another foreign country with lagging wage rates. Relative parity in wage rates around the world is a long way off.

IN THIS DAY OF AUTOMATED FACTORIES, it is difficult to understand the continued attraction of offshore operations, but for the existence of the foreign subsidiary tax loophole.

In certain low-tech industries, like the needle trades, the attraction of lower offshore wages could be understood if not liked. Increased transportation costs would not have been a significant offsetting factor. In other industries, the cost of shipping heavy products back to the United States would have been a material

---

* See "*Offshore Outsourcing's Next Wave: How High?*" by Steve Lohr, The New York Times, February 14, 2008.

factor in offsetting the offshore wage differential. None of this applies to the new high tech products (think digital) which are relatively small, don't weigh much, and are manufactured in highly automated plants where workers play a lesser role.

The United States has the ability to build sophisticated automated factories, has the know-how, and has competent workers. Higher US wage costs, to the extent that they still exist, would be less of a factor in such automated factories. Raw materials are readily available in the United States, probably more so and cheaper than offshore.

It is beginning to look like the US foreign subsidiary tax loophole is becoming more and more of the fundamental rationale for those offshore operations, making the elimination of the loophole more and more important.

The accelerating growth of high-tech capabilities in foreign countries, which comes in significant part at the expense of a diminishing US domestic economic base, cannot be in the interest of the United States. It virtually cries for Congress to eliminate the US tax incentive for offshore operations.

One has to wonder about how the US economic scene would look today if the manufacture of digital and other high-tech products hadn't been shifted offshore decades ago. The least Congress can do today is to close the foreign subsidiary loophole.

Chapter 4

Moving Research & Know-How Offshore

American know-how and research & development will shape the future wellbeing of the United States. The US education system provides the human raw material, but it is know-how and R&D that gets the job done. Government agencies like the National Institute of Health might get a project off the ground, but it is in the factories, laboratories, and other facilities of American companies where the meaningful concrete advances are made. Those facilities might relocate offshore with adverse long-term consequences, and the United States provides a tax incentive (the foreign subsidiary loophole) for US companies to do just that.

THE TRANSFER OF AMERICAN KNOW-HOW OFFSHORE necessarily flows from the commencement of manufacturing offshore. There could be good business reasons for manufacturing offshore, particularly if it is to serve that foreign market. Manufacturing know-how might be generally available today it is just a question of time when the foreign country will have it, if it does not already have it.

However, there can be some specialized know-how that is unique and critical to an industry where protecting it can crucial to keeping competition at bay. For instance, wing construction know-how was once critical in the airframe manufacturing industry. To be sure, any type of know-how would be developed by others in time, but, by that time, the initial developer might have advanced to new and better ways to do things.

LOCATING R&D ACTIVITIES OFFSHORE could be accelerating. Some of it could be artificial or make-believe if it is just the financial engineers needing to conduct R&D in a tax-haven so as to intangibles there, in order to divert income there. That is not like conducting R&D on the French Riviera because the best researchers and scientists could be attracted to work for the company there.*

The importance of R&D in this day and age is recognized by some governments adopting competitive programs to attract or force the conduct of R&D activities within their boundaries. A deal requiring the conduct of R&D within the country could be the quid pro quo for that country allowing a business enterprise of another country to commence local operations. Such deals wouldn't be transparent or made known, but could exist.

A country could have publically known policies or programs to attract companies that are likely to conduct R&D locally or are so high-tech that the product line itself would inform.

---

* Along this line, see "*From I.B.M. Jobs to Assignments in Paris*," Penny Singer, The New York Times, March 1, 1992.

China has a 25% tax-rate but offers a lower 15% tax-rate to attract new-tech and high-tech enterprises and certain integrated circuits production enterprises while the US tax system operates to induce US companies to go offshore and accept such offers. Together they dovetail beautifully, but neither is the US national interest.

The US has a tax-incentive for R&D, namely a meager and severely limited R&D credit against the US income tax of a company conducting business in the United States. The United States does not seem to have any affirmative program to attract R&D to within its borders. The least it can do is to stop the US tax incentive to operate abroad (plug the foreign subsidiary loophole), which would serve to eliminate the concomitant US incentive to conduct R&D activities abroad.

Four years ago a paper was published in The New England Journal of Medicine, the leading medical publication in the United States, addressing the "Ethical and Scientific Implications of the Globalization of Clinical Research" and raising questions about conducting clinical trials offshore.[*] The problems were apparently growing as shown by the percentage of FDA registered investigator based in the United States having declined from 86 percent to 54 percent of the total registered in the ten years ending in 2007. Back in 2005 it was noted that China and India were starting to spend heavily in biotechnology and that Singapore built scientist-attracting research centers.[†]

It seems that all the developed countries, particularly the ones with good educational systems, have a variety of grants, funding arrangements and other incentives for the R&D areas they consider important. The poorer or lesser-developed countries don't have the money to do this and probably don't have the educated people needed in R&D, nor could they attract them; their

---

[*] "*Outsourcing of Drug Trials Is Faulted*," Natasha Singer, The New York Times, February 19, 2009.

[†] "*Medical Companies Joining Offshore Trend*," Andrew Pollack, The New York Times, February 24, 2005.

interest being in obtaining jobs currently for their unemployed workers. The larger, more developed nations can afford to look to the future more.

As things develop, perhaps R&D competition might yield to R&D co-operation. It could become a two-way street in time with nations getting as much as they are giving. A large Swiss drug company relocated its research headquarters from Switzerland to the United States to be near US universities and near American companies working in the same field.* Whether this gives as much as it takes is unknown, but it's probably a two-way street to some extent.

This is the cutting edge and it will develop as it will. Whatever the course for the United States, it is clear that the United States should stop giving a tax incentive for US companies to shift or commence R&D activities offshore by plugging the foreign subsidiary loophole.

Plugging the loophole would also serve to eliminate the attraction of lower-tax rates or tax holidays being offered by foreign countries to attract high-tech and scientifically oriented industries, defeating the value of such programs.

DISASTROUS CONSEQUENCES CAN FOLLOW from the development of valuable property rights offshore. R&D conducted offshore in foreign subsidiaries can lead to patents and other intangibles property rights being owned by those subsidiaries. A foreign subsidiary would own the worldwide patent rights to any invention made by it, even the patent rights in the United States. And those foreign subsidiaries could be taken-over or expropriated by the foreign government.

---

* "*Medical Companies Joining Offshore Trend*," Andrew Pollack, The New York Times, February 24, 2005.

The foreign subsidiary would have been incorporated under the laws of the foreign country where it is located. As such, the foreign subsidiary could be viewed as a national of that country, subject to whatever control and influence that foreign government would care to exercise over it.

The rule of law does not always prevail, and over the decades there is no telling what might transpire. The foreign government could take control of the foreign subsidiary and manage it and its patents, or interfere in any way it wants. It would be like a sovereign dealing with its national. There is always the risk of outright expropriation.

Issues might arise in a third country where patents were obtained as to whether the expropriating country would be recognized as the effective owner of those patents. If the US parent doesn't prevail in wresting ownership of the patents, it would have lost key assets and have created a new competitor at the same time. So what started for tax reduction purposes can lead to disastrous consequences.

Also, there is no telling what changing world conditions might lead to. Bayer, the German pharmaceutical company, had to buy back the right to use its own name in the United States after it had been expropriated (along with its patents) during World War I. Jarring scenarios do arise from time to time.

The best place for a US company to conduct R&D and own the fruits of that R&D has to be the United States. Closing the foreign subsidiary loophole would kill the US tax inducement to do otherwise.

Chapter 5

Moving Intangibles Offshore

As the foreign subsidiary loophole provides US companies with advantageous tax treatment of their offshore earnings, there is an incentive to maximize those offshore earnings by moving intangibles offshore. Simply put, foreign subsidiary ownership of intangible rights allows the foreign subsidiary to license those rights to unrelated parties and increase offshore profits. Those intangible rights can also be licensed to affiliated companies with an aim to reducing the foreign taxes the affiliates are subject to. The more valuable the intangible rights the greater the royalties to be earned and the greater the potential foreign tax reduction.

GETTING THE INTANGIBLE RIGHTS INTO THE FOREIGN SUBSIDIARY is the main problem encountered by the US parent company. The transfer of an intangible to a foreign subsidiary is considered a US taxable event. It is considered a sale at fair market value which, for a valuable intangible, can be enormous. As the costs of developing intangibles are usually tax deductible immediately when incurred, the taxpayer would not normally have any cost basis in the transferred intangible right and the entire sales price (the full fair market value) would be taxable.

The transfer itself could take various forms and still be considered a sale resulting in the recognition of US taxable income. For instance, the contribution of intangible rights upon the initial incorporation of the foreign subsidiary in exchange for foreign subsidiary stock is considered a sale. Allowing a foreign subsidiary to take out a patent on the US parent company's newly developed product would be treated as a transfer of rights and considered a sale.

While values can be argued, the endeavor is to somehow avoid the issue entirely by structuring the transfer of the intangible rights in such a way that it is not considered to be a taxable event or that there was no transfer (that is, the foreign subsidiary itself created the intangible).

Various subterfuges are used depending on the intangible rights to be transferred. Frequently the transfer of an intangible takes place as an early stage in the development process where the value isn't clear, or a claim can be made that there is no value, or there is a better chance that the matter is overlooked or buried.

The transfer of a trade name seems to get a free ride when the name of the US parent company is used in naming the foreign subsidiary. Decades ago it might have been successfully argued that the name, in English, means nothing in the foreign language and thus has no value. This probably changed with globalization and the advent of the internet, telephone satellites, videos and worldwide media. Now, trade names (the company name) and trademarks (the name or logo that gets stamped on the product itself) might be known throughout the world, whatever the local language. That could make transfers difficult. And a trademark, with its indeterminable life as contrasted to a very limited life for a patent, could be the most valuable intangible of all.

One might wonder how some intangible rights wind up in a foreign subsidiary incorporated in an unexpected place, usually a tax-haven country. The advantage of having intangibles located in a tax-haven subsidiary revolves around the income produced by the intangible bring taxed at a low rate or not taxed at all by the tax-haven country.

Tax-haven counties are not generally known to be locations for conducting research, development or sales activities that produce valuable intangibles. Thus, it is likely that either the valuable intangibles found housed in these tax-haven subsidiaries had been transferred into the subsidiary or that very sophisticated ways had been found to create the intangibles within the tax-haven subsidiary itself.

Financial engineers excel at this, but management should be aware that the matter can be challenged by the tax authorities and losing the issue can result in a huge tax. This is a real risk, a risk that management must take if the company is to play the tax game.

However, it should be recognized that the tax game might not be worth the candle even if the tax authority challenge proves to be unsuccessful. Also worth considering is that the tax game disappears when the foreign subsidiary loophole that created the tax advantage is closed; which has to happen sooner or later (see the chapter "*Combating Offshore Plundering -- Closing the Foreign Subsidiary Loophole*").

TAX GAMING WITH INTANGIBLES is part of the financial engineer's art. "Intangibles" include all sorts of incorporeal or intellectual property rights like patents, trademarks, copyrights, and trade names to take the most common. The term might even be extended to designs, procedures, exclusivity agreements and whatever else the financial engineers can contrive.

These rights have value, frequently substantial value. The owner of such rights has the right, if not the tax obligation, to charge for the use of the intangible rights by another party. The other party could be unrelated or it could be a related party within the affiliated group. If a US parent company owns worldwide patent rights, it not only has the right to charge its foreign subsidiary for using the patent, it has an obligation under the US tax laws to do so.

The United States insists that the profits of each affiliated company in the group be fairly determined. Thus, if one corporate entity in a multinational group sells products to another corporate entity in the group, the product must be sold at a fair price. Since there could be two taxing jurisdictions involved, and there usually are, it would be easy to shift profits from one taxing jurisdiction to the other by merely selling intercompany at a higher or lower price. Determining the fair price may be, and usually is, difficult but that remains the universal standard to be enforced by taxing authority audits.

A similar rule applies to the intercompany use of intangibles. A fair royalty or other consideration must be obtained. Again, it would be easy to distort reported profits in the multinational locations by charging a higher or lower royalty or charging no royalty at all. The amount of the royalty is determined by the corporate owner of the intangible rights, subject to audit for fairness by the tax authorities involved. The company's CPAs are also involved as they too have an interest in separate entity accounting statements being fairly stated.

A tax-haven subsidiary might function in a sales capacity based on sales agreements, representation agreements or other such agreements that might be viewed as creating some sort of intangible right in the tax-haven. If a valuable right were being transferred to the tax-haven subsidiary, it should be charged a fair price for the right transferred and it, in turn, should charge a fair intercompany price when exercising that right.

For example, granting an exclusive right to sell a product might have independent value, with the contractual right being capable of being sold for a consideration; that is, sold at a price, for cash. Or the exclusive right might be granted to a recipient in exchange for various contractual commitments by the recipient relating to the sale of the product. It all depends on the value and demand for the product itself, and the market position of the contractual party (reputation, following, experience) and the extent of its sales staff and facilities. The question would be what independent parties would charge/pay for exclusive sales rights or barter for a grant of exclusivity?

A mere paper operation, not supported by any ownership of intangible rights, would not stand up. For instance, in a paper billing operation, the tax-haven subsidiary cuts a purchase order to the US parent (or other affiliated company that produces the product) at one price, and then cuts an invoice selling the product at a higher price to an unrelated or another affiliated company, booking the mark-up as a profit earned in the tax-haven country while having the product shipped directly from the producer to the purchaser and doing nothing else. This is an obvious sham, lacking any substance, and won't stand up.

Financial engineers would build much more substance into their arrangements. The tip off for tax authority audits would be high tax-haven profits produced with minimal expense and activity.

The issue of fairness in intercompany (or "transfer") pricing always exists. The prices or fees charged between affiliates can always be challenged by the tax authorizes of any of the countries involved as being either too high or too low depending on which direction the supposed profit diversion takes place. For example, the price paid to the US parent company for the product might be too low (diverting profit out of the United

States to the tax-haven), and the re-sale price to an affiliated company in Germany might be too high (diverting profit out of Germany to the tax-haven).

Sometimes the tax authorities are successful in their challenges. However, the better bet is that the tax authorities are understaffed with the result being that many arrangements are not audited, and, if there happens to be an audit, that the tax auditor is not all that competent with issues being missed or not argued effectively.

THE FOREIGN SUBSIDIARY LOOPHOLE is behind the various ways US companies reduce foreign taxes, because the effort to do so wouldn't be worthwhile if the loophole hadn't been created. Closing the foreign subsidiary loophole drives this book. Closing the loophole destroys the value of all the foreign tax-reduction strategies.

Wondrous arrangements* serve to reduce taxes. Congress might have unknowingly created the foreign subsidiary loophole, but today it has to be knowingly continued by Congress to the point where it is destroying the US economic base. Taxpayers have the right, and some would say the duty, to keep their taxes at a minimum. Others would say it has gone too far. President Ronald Reagan once said things had gone too far and proceeded to close tax loopholes.†

The purpose here is not to delineate the various tactics used to reduce foreign tax, nor can the full gamut ever be known.

---

* The media recently referred to and perhaps was having fun with a "Double Irish With a Dutch Sandwich" that was apparently coupled with a Caribbean twist. See "*How Apple Sidesteps Billions in Taxes*," by Charles Duhigg and David Kocieniewski, The New York Times, April 28, 2012, and "*Inquiry Into Tech Giants' Tax Strategies Nears End*," by Charles Duhigg and David Kocieniewski, The New York Times, January 3, 2013.

† "G.E.'s Strategies Let It Avoid Taxes Altogether," by David Kocieniewski, The New York Times, March 24, 2011.

Rather, the purpose is to show that in all instances it is the existence of the foreign subsidiary loophole that creates the incentive to reduce foreign taxes. Had all foreign subsidiaries been included in the US tax returns of the US parent companies, as the US worldwide tax system would demand, there would be little or no incentive to reduce foreign taxes and time and attention would be redirected to business matters.

Thus, a change in the US tax laws to require current inclusion of all foreign subsidiaries in the US tax returns of the US parent companies would render the tax-reduction structures useless and probably lead to their unwinding and getting back to business.

In addition, plugging the loophole would assist top management, if it is of the mind to do so, in getting off the tax treadmill. With things getting out of hand and with US company managements appearing in the press to be anything but good corporate citizens, some managements might want the loophole plugged or might not oppose the loophole closing.

Foreign governments have also become concerned with the situation.[*] Their viewing a company as not being a good corporate citizen could impact other facets of that company's relations with that government and also impact the inter-government relations of the United States itself. Ethically, the US government should be concerned with US companies skirting foreign taxes to the point where foreign governments complain.

This matter is addressed in detail in the next chapter "*Ethical Considerations in US Foreign Policy and in Company Offshore Activities.*" Suffice it to say at this point that US foreign policy is neither immoral nor amoral but is morally and ethically based. The US moral/ethical stance extends to the offshore activities of American corporations.

---

* "*European Countries Seek More Taxes From U.S. Multinational Companies,*" by Eric Pfanner, The New York Times, November 18, 2012.

Chapter 6

Ethical Considerations in US Foreign Policy and in Company Offshore Activities

Some 40 years ago, a high-level presidential adviser wrote an article entitled "*The Necessary Amorality of Foreign Affairs*."* Attitudes must have changed somewhat about 30 years later as the title was changed to "*Is There a Place for Morality in Foreign Affairs?*" when the article was reprinted in a compendium.† The article maintained that morality was irrelevant in foreign affairs and should be disregarded.

---

* By Arthur Schlesinger, Jr., Harper's, August 1971.

† "*An American Album, One Hundred and Fifty Years of Harper's Magazine*," Lewis H. Lapham, Editor, foreword by Arthur Schlesinger, Jr., LPC Group, New York, April 1, 2000. Only inconsequential textual changes appeared in the article.

Doing what is perceived to be best for the nation appeared to be the standard even though the action itself could be considered immoral. We can debate what was then best for the nation and whether we were in fact being immoral or amoral, but today there is no doubt. Today, there is a clear moral imperative in what we do, both in our foreign policy and with respect to the offshore activities of US companies.

BEING A GOOD CORPORATE CITIZENS throughout the world is the standard to which US companies are held. We want our companies to do appear to do what is right, and do good, earning respect for them and for the United States. This is where the national interest resides today, as reflected in laws passed by our Congress.

For instance, consider the existing US laws concerning offshore bribery. A US parent company cannot allow its foreign subsidiaries bribe foreign officials even though bribery might be an acceptable local practice and even though bribery might result in increased offshore profits. Congress deemed it best to favor a strict moral code and forego any possible benefit flowing from an immoral or amoral code of conduct. The matter was considered serious enough to make it a criminal penalty in the United States even though the criminal bribery takes place abroad.

Congress saw fit to enact the law even though that law could and surely would weaken the ability of US companies to operate and compete abroad. It was more important for American companies be viewed as, and in fact be, good corporate citizens abroad just like we insist that they be good corporate citizens domestically.

There is obviously an ethical bias underlying the public policy of the United States against foreign bribery. The simple proposition is that we should not have lower standards abroad.

"IN ROME, DO WHAT THE ROMANS DO." This mantra, frequently heard, contradicts the ethical stance. There is logic behind doing what the locals do in matters like crossing the street and in other day-to-day living matters. But in matters of ethics and in the business context generally, we shouldn't seek to do what the locals do, but rather maintain our standards.

As guests of the foreign country, we should not pollute the land even though the locals do so. We know better, we don't pollute at home, and we are not poor like the locals who have no other option but pollute their own land. It is not a matter of imposing our standards on others but adhering to our own standards. Our companies should go abroad to do business, not to take advantage of things we know to be bad.

Today, the ethical imperative goes beyond what the US parent company sanctions in the operation of a plant owned by its foreign subsidiary. US companies are also being called to task when they have their products manufactured for them by independent suppliers who do not match up to American standards.

The local suppliers own and manage the factories, and hire and supervise the workers. They would likely adhere to local standards to the same extent that others in their community do, skirting local laws as other locals do, and they might pursue practices that would embarrass American managers trained under much higher US standards.

Matters like using child labor, having sweat shop conditions, forcing excessive worker overtime, violating local laws and providing unsafe work conditions could lead to criticism of the US company even though it is merely buying products produced by an unrelated supplier following accepted local practices.

The criticism originates with the US media that tends to reflect the strong feelings Americans have about such matters when brought to their attention. The pressure arises back home where the US company's products are sold. The company losses respect, and a hot button event brought to the public's attention triggers censure and derision. It could impact domestic sales or even lead to demonstrations or boycotts having a more exhibitable impact on sales.

Fundamentally, it is the ethical stance of the American public that is being displayed. The US company is being taken to account for both direct missteps on its own part and also for its failure to act where it is in a position to act. This exhibits that Americans do indeed have high ethical standards. Even higher, if the American public is viewed as a partial beneficiary of products produced at a lower cost offshore. Their ethical posture leads to higher prices for them as cleaning up the suppliers act will be at a cost, but yet Americans insist on ethical conduct abroad.

This potentially casts US companies into new rolls abroad. They would not ordinarily seek to improve worker conditions in plants not owned by them. They would not normally aspire to police the enforcement of local laws.

But still, the US company would not be imposing its standards offshore. Rather, in taking its foreign supplier to task,* the US company would be pursuing what it considers to be its own social responsibility, and in full recognition that its costs will increase. It could also be viewed as acceptance of the ethical bent and rejection of amoral or immoral conduct in offshore operations.

NEGOTIATING A FOREIGN TAX HOLIDAY is legal, but can be heart rendering when fully understood. In the scenario being addressed, a US company approaches a foreign government demanding a tax holiday if it were to establish manufacturing operations within its borders.

It becomes heart rendering when a destitute or extremely poor foreign country is involved. Such a country needs tax

* See "*Signs of Changes Taking Hold in Electronics Factories in China*," by Keith Bradsher and Charles Duhigg, The New York Times, December 26, 2012.

revenues as much as they need jobs for their people. A strong ethical case can be made for not depriving them of what would normally flow to them under the circumstances.

The US company's demand would effectively amount to extortion if it already decided to establish offshore operations in that country, which can easily be the case and probably is the case. That the demand is extortion cannot be known to the foreign government and responded to on that basis, since the government might not be savvy or have the needed information.

There is much more to the location of a plant than the applicable taxes. Labor costs and the availability of labor of the skill levels required could outweigh taxation. Availability of raw materials and proximity to markets would also be important. So would political stability.

It's never a fair negotiation when a large sophisticated company negotiates for a special deal. The poorer the country, the less tuned-in their politicians. And the local politicians have everything to gain on the personal level from entering into a deal, any deal. They become heroes for attracting jobs, job that they overpaid for and would have gotten anyway.

Even if the foreign government should assemble a sufficient package to make it "worthwhile" to the potential investor to invest locally, the investor rarely commits to specifics like the number of jobs and how long the investor will stay.

The elimination of the foreign subsidiary loophole will help these poor countries in that it minimalizes the value of any tax holiday to a US company. What would otherwise be saved locally in terms of local income taxes would flow to the US Treasury, reducing the incentive for the US company to seek it.

However, plugging the US foreign subsidiary loophole will not stop extortion if the US company is of that mind. The US company could ask for cash subsidies (that would be hard to get in the poorer countries) or exemptions from local laws or demand special privileges. And it would not be surprising for a signed deal not to bind the company as the number of jobs wouldn't always be specified and the company would normally be free to close or move the plant elsewhere.

The only pressure that could be brought to bear on the US company to curtail such demands would be bad press in the United States about their not being a good corporate citizen. The vigilance of US media and the good judgment of aware Americans would be needed along with Congress closing the tax loophole.

DOMESTICALLY, ON THE STATE AND LOCAL LEVEL, the same type of extortion could take place when a new plant is to be built. There is job competition between the States, even between the cities, and once again the local politicians are far outclassed as negotiators by the potential investor.

The locals would not know whether they would be the favored local anyway, they wouldn't able to bind the investor to specifics as to employment and remaining over time, and they would be under political pressure to get the boded jobs whatever the price to be paid. The price could include State income tax exemptions and credits, exemptions or reductions in sales and property taxes, free services, cash grants and loans and other type of special aid.

Those incentives were recently estimated to amount to $80 billion, with some Federal Reserve Bank economists showing that the incentives did not, like a zero sum game, increase overall economic value.* A single grant can be over $100 million in cash, and a tax credit over the years can amount to over a billion dollars. Even with those huge amounts being paid, one has to wonder whether it can truly drive multi-billion dollar investments where location advantages, transportation costs, labor skill levels and

* "*As Companies Seek Tax Deals, Governments Pay High Price*," By Louise Story, The New York Times, December 1, 2012.

availability, and raw material availability would normally be paramount, making the whole incentive game no more than extortion if these factors drive the investment decision.

Fortunately, something can be done legally in the United States to curtail this without having to rely on the company being a good corporate citizen. About 6 years ago, the Supreme Court threw out a taxpayer lawsuit against a discriminatory incentive because the taxpayer did not have legal status. Future litigants might have status, and there could be other ways to stop this zero-sum game.

It might be possible to design Federal legislation, based on the Interstate Commerce clause or otherwise, to forbid such discriminatory practices. Any practice that operates to favor a specific party or group, or turns out to apply to a limited few, could forbidden. Coupling this with closing the foreign subsidiary loophole would help counter the argument that the extortionists would just move jobs overseas if they didn't get their subsidies.

COMBATING TAX LOOPHOLES AS THEY ARISE should become an ethical imperative. It should be high on the list of legislative activities for both the Executive and Legislative branches of our government lest the tax burden be unfairly shifted to make up the shortfall created by the loophole. It is a question of fairness and equity, not just one of enforcing the law.

The alternative is the erosion of the US tax base and annual battles to balance the budget by placing the burden of the revenue shortfall on others, or the alternative is in increasing the debt to be paid by future generations. Ideally, there should be an annual endeavor to close emerging loopholes, whatever the expected political opposition.

It is noted that special tax benefits and tax loopholes loom wider and bigger when placed in an international context. An extraordinary $100 million in assets can be housed in an individual retirement account (an IRA) designed for an average person's wages. By investing IRA funds in a foreign corporation or otherwise structured by a financial engineer, the IRA's 35% unrelated business-income tax can be avoided; showing how esoteric the international context can get.*

This is the level of tax planning sold by financial engineers to legitimate investors who feel that they are complying with the US tax laws. The investors cannot be expected to fully understand what they are being advised or the ramifications to the nation if everyone did the same (the categorical imperative).

It is legitimate for individuals to keep their taxes to a minimum, so the blame rests with the successive Administrations and Congresses not keeping up with tax-reduction ploys and stopping them. Emerging loophole of any stripe should be closed legislatively as arise and became known to Administration tax policy people or Congressional staffers.

The simple answer is that more legislative attention should be paid to tax matters as distasteful and controversial as that might be in Washington; before the loopholes get of hand, before tax revenues are severely impacted. Waiting for the courts to close loopholes by litigating makes no sense. Once something is decided to be a loophole and the decision is reached to litigate, the loophole should also be attacked legislatively.

---

* Op-Ed piece "*Mitt Romney's Financial Mysteries*," by Michael Graetz, The New York Times, July 30, 2012.

Chapter 7

Shareholder Accounting for Offshore Operations (GAAP)

"GAAP" stands for Generally Accepted Accounting Principles used for shareholder accounting purposes, SEC filings and the like. It is aimed at fairly measuring corporate earnings reported to shareholders. GAAP accounting is to be distinguished from tax accounting used in the preparation of tax returns designed to report taxable income to the US Treasury in accordance with the Internal Revenue Code.

Both GAAP and tax accounting would include the earnings of a foreign branch of a US company. In using a foreign branch, the US company operates directly in its own name without interposing a foreign subsidiary to conduct the offshore operations. All the earnings of the US company would be taxed current by the United States with the US Treasury giving a credit for foreign taxes paid by the branch. The foreign tax credit* is covered in the next chapter "*Avoiding Double Taxation -- The US Foreign Tax Credit System*."

The situation changes when a foreign subsidiary is interposed to conduct the offshore operation. The GAAP accounting earnings reported to shareholders and the SEC would remain the same. However, due to the foreign subsidiary loophole, the earnings of the foreign subsidiary would not be included for tax accounting purposes and accordingly would not be included in US parent company's US tax return. Thus, the US Treasury would not collect any US tax on the foreign earnings. It would not collect the $10 tax in the footnote example.

In the foreign subsidiary situation, the GAAP accounting reports would still include the $10 US tax on the foreign earnings as a current expense because that tax would be due and payable to the US Treasury if and when the foreign subsidiary pays up its earnings as dividends to the US parent company. It is called a "deferred" tax because actual payment to the US Treasury awaits a future event, but the deferred tax must be charged to earnings currently. The deferred tax depresses reported earnings in the same period the pre-tax earnings are reported to shareholders. This is the only way to fairly measure and report current earnings.

To do otherwise would distort reported earnings in two accounting periods. Otherwise, current period GAAP accounting would not reflect all the expenses associated with earning the income currently reported (the first distortion), and the required

---

* Where the foreign tax-rate is 25%, foreign branch earnings of $100 would be subject to a $25 foreign tax. With a 35% US tax-rate, the US tax on the $100 of branch earnings would be $35. To avoid double taxation, the United States would give a foreign tax credit of $25 for the foreign tax and thus collect only $10 of US tax (35 - 25 = 10) on the foreign earnings.
The total tax on the foreign earnings would amount to $35 ($25 foreign and $10 US), which effectively subjects the foreign earning to the same tax-rate as domestic earnings (35%) and produces tax-neutrality between foreign and domestic operations. All the taxes would be due currently.

payment of the tax would depress earnings in a later period when the intercompany dividend is paid (the second distortion). An intercompany dividend does not give rise to GAAP income, so the later period would just reflect the tax with no income reported.

Reflecting the deferred taxes as a current charge against reported earnings does not vitiate the benefit the US company derives from the foreign subsidiary loophole. The US company still manages to report to shareholders all its income wherever earned, while excluding some of that income from reports to the US tax collector. It is not a bad arrangement if you can get it, and the US company can get it by merely placing the offshore operation in a voluntarily created intermediary foreign subsidiary.

"DEFERRED" TAX is the accounting label given to the tax to be paid the US Treasury in the future when the foreign subsidiary remits its earnings as dividends to the US parent company. The deferred tax is set up on the books of account as a liability owed the US Treasury. In accounting parlance, there is a ($10)"debit" on the profit and loss statement reducing reported earnings and a ($10)"credit" on the balance sheet showing the future tax as an outstanding liability to the US Treasury.

As is the case with any other liability shown on a company's balance sheet (like accounts payable), there is no charge to earning when the liability is actually paid. When the foreign subsidiary pays its earnings up to its US parent company as a dividend, the US parent company pays off its balance sheet liability to the US Treasury without charging earnings.

Thus, if the US parent company wanted to bring up some foreign subsidiary cash home by having the foreign subsidiary pay a dividend, some of that cash would go to pay the deferred tax liability to the US Treasury but there would be no charge to earnings. Similarly, if Congress should eliminate the foreign subsidiary loophole and require that the US parent company then pay the deferred tax liability, there would be no charge to earnings even if the cash came from foreign subsidiary dividends.

THE "PERMANENTLY REINVESTED" EXCEPTION to the normal deferred tax accounting rules allows the US parent company to skip recording some deferred taxes. The exception is based on the proposition that a foreign subsidiary permanently reinvesting its earnings in its operations would not have those earnings available to pay dividends and thus the US parent company need not record deferred tax expense.

The permanent reinvested exception is an accounting concept that serves only to determine whether deferred taxes should be set up on the company books. It is not a tax concept that would serve to free otherwise taxable income from tax merely because the taxable income would be permanently reinvested in the business.

The CPAs who certify the US parent company's financial statements could strictly interpret this exception by requiring hard evidence that the earnings have been or clearly are committed to be permanently reinvested offshore. This would be in contrast to merely accepting a declared intention to permanently reinvest offshore, which is discussed below.

Hard evidence would include an investment in land or a commitment to purchase land, or say an investment in additional inventories need to support the growing sales volume the foreign subsidiary enjoys. It would not appear to apply to the accumulated cash hoard that could be used for anything. All there could be with accumulated cash would be an intention or plan to reinvest, which is discussed below.

Even where the hard evidence existed, conditions might change in the future requiring withdrawal from that investment, potentially triggering a charge to earnings for the US tax at that time. That risk is unlikely to be as great as the risk of Congress changing the law, with a negative effect on the quality of earnings.

The amount of permanently reinvested foreign earning on which US tax had not been recorded might or might not be disclosed in financial statements and SEC filings. The need to disclose could vary based on how the matter is viewed and the materiality of amount. It is not known whether any researcher has made an estimate of the aggregate amount of US tax not so recorded as deferred taxes on the accounting statements of US parent companies. Not recording such deferred taxes increases profits reported to shareholders and thus provides an even greater incentive for offshore operations and expanding offshore operations under the foreign subsidiary loophole.

THE "INTENTION" TO PERMANENTLY REINVEST OFFSHORE becomes a tricky matter because there wouldn't normally be any hard evidence to support an intention or a plan. Intentions and plans can change at any time, even firm intentions and written plans. US parent companies arguing for a repatriation tax holiday would deny the existence of a firm intention to permanently reinvest abroad.

Had no deferred US tax been provided on the $300 billion brought back under the last repatriation tax holiday, there would have been no accounting windfall profit appearing on the shareholder financial statements. The intention to reinvest offshore would have proven to be short-lived instead of permanent, the required charge to earning being avoided by the tax holiday.

The permanently reinvested determination would appear to be a difficult one for the accountants, perhaps somewhat similar to dealing with the inclusion or exclusion of special purpose financing vehicles in the accounting consolidations that have been troublesome in the past as in the Enron situation.

This book generally puts aside the permanently reinvested exception to keep things simple by focusing only the existence of deferred taxes having been set up on the accounting books. To the extent that the permanent reinvestment exception was used, it should be kept in mind that there is the risk of the US parent company having to charge earnings if the reinvestment unexpectedly proves not to be permanent or if Congress repeals the foreign subsidiary loophole as could be expected sooner or later.

FORGIVING A DEFERRED TAX that had reduced reported profits in prior periods would result in an increase reported profits at the time payment is forgiven. We see this when companies settle their taxes for a prior period with the IRS for less than they had initially estimated and recorded on their books of account -- an increase in profits is usually reported currently instead of restating the old years to reflect the lower tax.

Forgiving deferred taxes can arise from Congress passing a repatriation tax holiday or from a basic change in law like the adoption of a territorial tax system. These matters are discussed in detail in the chapter "*Combating Offshore Plundering -- Closing the Foreign Subsidiary Loophole.*"

Reporting a tremendous windfall profit on the shareholder accounting statements provides additional motivation to undertake efforts to get the deferred taxes forgiven. Those deferred taxes amount to hundreds of billions of dollars, which would represent a humongous windfall profit for those who went offshore. A large company could have a windfall amounting to billions of dollar.

It is called a windfall profit because it would be in the nature of a handout, freebie, or giveaway. Critics could view the pursuit of such a windfall profit as adding insult to injury; the injury of moving US jobs aboard, hurting the US economy and of contributing to domestic budget and deficit problems. Some critics could call arguing for it chutzpah.

Chapter 8

Avoiding Double Taxation -- The US Foreign Tax Credit System

There is a danger of double taxation when a corporation conducts operations in two countries: both the home and host countries could tax the profit earned in an offshore operation.

The danger of double taxation exists whether the American company conducts the offshore operation directly in its own name through a branch or, instead, houses the offshore operation in a foreign subsidiary. Normally the subsidiary would be incorporated in the country where the foreign operation would be conducted; a Chinese subsidiary for operations to be conducted in China, an Irish subsidiary for operations conducted in Ireland and so forth.

With a foreign branch operation, the income earned in the branch would be taxable currently by both the United States and the foreign host country. With a foreign subsidiary operation, the foreign country would tax the profit earned currently and the

United State would tax the profit when the subsidiary remits the profits earned as dividends to the US parent company. The US foreign tax credit system was designed to avoid double taxation in both situations.

THE OPERATION OF THE US FOREIGN TAX CREDIT system is not difficult to understand.* Paying a double tax on the same pre-tax income would be an intolerable burden on the American company and would unwisely deter offshore operations that would be established for good business reasons. The US foreign tax credit mechanism was designed to allow American companies to operate offshore, free of the burden of double taxation.

The host country where the profit is earned is considered to have the primary right to tax the income earned within it boarders, so it is up to home country (the United States) to reduce its taxes so as to avoid double taxation. Thus, under a foreign tax credit mechanism, the home country allows a credit against its tax on the offshore income for the amount of foreign tax paid the host

---

* Take a simple situation of an offshore branch earning $100 in pre-tax profit for the year and the foreign country (the "host" country) having a 25% tax-rate and levying a $25 (100 x 0.25 = 25) tax on that profit. Assume that the United States (the "home" country) has a 35% tax-rate and would levy a tax on the offshore branch income of $35 (100 x 0.35 = 35). The total taxes on the offshore income would amount to $60 (25 + 35 = 60) if there were no foreign tax credit.

Under the foreign tax credit system, the United States would give a $25 credit against the $35 in US tax due on the same profit and would collect only $10 in US tax. The total taxes on the offshore income would amount to $35 (25 + 10 = 35). Thus, the taxpayer winds up paying the higher (35%) of the two tax-rates under the foreign tax credit system.

Instead, had the foreign tax-rate been higher, say 45%, $45 in tax would have been paid to the foreign country. The US tax of $35 at its 35% tax-rate would be offset by a foreign tax credit of $35 because the United States limits the credit to the US tax-rate (35%). Thus, the United States would collect no US tax on the offshore income, and the taxpayer winds up paying the higher (45%) of the two tax-rates.

country; the credit is a direct dollar-for-dollar reduction in tax, not merely a deduction used in computing tax.

As a result of this mechanism, the offshore profit is burdened with the higher of the foreign or US tax-rate. The United States does not provide a credit for foreign tax in excess of the US tax on the offshore income. The following table portrays what happens at various foreign tax-rate scenarios.

Assume a 35% United States Tax Rate						
	25% Foreign Tax Rate		35% Foreign Tax Rate		45% Foreign Tax Rate	
Pre-tax profit		$100		$100		$100
US Tax	$35		$35		$35	
less credit	-25	10	-35	0	-35	0
Foreign tax		25		35		45
Total tax		35		35		45
After-tax profit		$65		$65		$55

FOREIGN SUBSIDIARY earnings get the same foreign tax credit treatment when the earnings are paid-up as a dividend to the US parent company. Computing the US tax on the dividend is more complex* but the net result exactly the same as with foreign branch earnings.

---

* Thus, if the foreign subsidiary earned $100 in pre-tax profit and paid $25 in foreign tax, US taxation would await the payment of a $75 dividend to the US parent, at which time the US Treasury would collect the $10 of deferred US tax. Had there been no US foreign tax credit, the US parent company would pay a full 35% tax on the $75 dividend it received, which would amount to $26 (75 x 0.35 = 26) in US tax.
A "gross-up" mechanism is used where, for US tax return computational purposes, the $25 in foreign tax that was paid by the foreign subsidiary (and reduced its dividend paying ability) is added back ("grossed-up") to the dividend actually paid ($75) to get back to the pre-tax profit ($100). Then the 35% US tax-rate is applied to the $100 of recomputed pre-tax profit, resulting in a $35 US tax that is reduced by the $25 foreign tax credit.
As a result, the United States collects only a $10 tax on the $75 dividend. That $10 would have been the amount of deferred US taxes recorded on the US parent company books of account kept for shareholder reporting purposes.

The difference between the US taxation of a foreign branch and a foreign subsidiary is strictly that of timing. The foreign branch earnings are taxed by the United States immediately, in the year the profit is earned. Taxing the earning of a foreign subsidiary is deferred to the time dividends are paid by the foreign subsidiary but the amount of deferred tax is recorded as an expense in the year the profit is earned.

Should a foreign subsidiary pay-out its earnings as dividends each year as they are earned, the tax situation would track that of a foreign branch. It is the interposition of a foreign corporate entity to conduct the offshore operation that creates the loophole allowing the deferral of the US tax until dividends are paid.

If a dividend is never paid, as only too often appears to be the case, the US Treasury will never collect the deferred tax due to it. Even if a dividend should sometimes be paid in the distant future, the US parent company would have delayed paying the tax for a substantial period of time, effectively getting an interest-free loan from the US Treasury for decades or more.

The Overall US Foreign Tax Credit

The computation of the US foreign tax credit on an overall basis presents another large loophole in the US international tax system. Under the overall computation, all foreign sourced taxable income is lumped together and all the foreign taxes are lumped together with a single foreign tax credit being computed.

Under a per-country computation, which is one of the alternatives to the overall computation, the taxable income sourced in a single foreign country and the taxes paid there determine the

US foreign tax credit for that country's taxes. A separate US foreign tax credit is computed for each country.

The table shown above illustrates how the foreign tax credit operates in the case of three different foreign tax rates. The table can also be used to illustrate how both the overall and the per-country US foreign tax credits operate. Assume that the US parent company has an offshore operation in each of three different foreign countries which have those different foreign tax-rates (25%, 35% and $45%).

The computed US foreign tax credits in the table are essentially per-country computations. A separate computation was made for each. In the first computation where the foreign tax-rate is 25%, the US Treasury collects $10 in US tax. In the second computation where the foreign tax-rate is the same as the same as the US tax-rate (35%), the US Treasury collects no tax. In the third computation, where the foreign tax-rate is 45%, the US Treasury also collects no tax. Add the three results; the US Treasury collects $10 in tax from the US parent company.

Instead, if the foreign income and taxes of the three operations were lumped together in an overall foreign tax credit computation, as is allowed today, the US Treasury collects nothing in tax from the US parent company. The higher tax incurred in the 45% tax-rate country balanced the lower tax in the 25% tax-rate country and averaged to 35%, which is equal to the US tax-rate and the US Treasury collects no tax.

Under the per-country computation, the US parent company would have had to pay the US Treasury the $10 owed in the first country computation. In the overall computation, that $10 needn't be paid because the $10 "extra" paid in the third country offset it. The tax burden of the higher tax rate (the "extra" $10) in the third country was shifted from the US parent company to the US Treasury under the overall computation. While the US foreign tax credit mechanism was aimed at limiting the US credit to the US tax-rate, the overall computation allowed the taxpayer to get a credit for a tax in excess of the US tax-rate.

JUSTIFYING THE OVERALL APPROACH is difficult. There is nothing inherent in a foreign tax credit system aimed at avoiding double taxation that requires the credit to be computed on an overall basis rather than a per-country basis. A per-country limitation would fulfill the purpose of the foreign tax credit and would make more theoretical and practical sense.

Also, it is the US parent company that chooses where to operate. It chose to operate in the high tax-rate country and it should to bear the burden of that decision. Fairness would dictate that the taxpayer bear the burden of its decisions. Providing an incentive for US companies to operate abroad is not fair to the American public, and the overall foreign tax credit computation adds to the inequity.

There is no taxpayer complexity or burden argument that can be directed at the per-country approach because the same information is required under either approach and computers make such considerations fall by the wayside.

A significant manipulation argument can me made against the overall approach as it allows both US parent companies and foreign governments to game the US tax system. For example, the foreign country could deliberately subject a local operation to a higher tax-rate knowing that its US parent company has offshore operations in other foreign countries with lower tax-rates that will offset their increased taxes. The US parent company could even prompt this if there is some special benefit to be obtained. To avoid appearing discriminatory, the higher tax-rate could be made applicable to a defined industry, with only one operation in that country meeting the definition.

More likely, the gaming would be in starting an offshore operation in the high tax-rate country that would otherwise not be justified, but the overall computation would have the US Treasury bear those higher taxes.

Still more likely, the gaming would be in the planning of dividends from the US parent company's offshore subsidiaries so as to reduce or eliminate the US tax due. Under the overall computation, the mix of dividends from the foreign subsidiaries could be designed to leave the US Treasury with no tax while the US parent let the low-taxed or non-taxed foreign earning accumulate offshore. And this is what is generally done.

The overall limitation also allows the mixing of different types of income to the disadvantage of the US Treasury. The foreign income referred to until now would be in the form of operating profits from a business being conducted offshore. A US parent company might also earn other type of income subject to foreign tax. For example, it might earn a cross-border royalty or a fee for some service that it renders. Cross-border income of this type is frequently subject to a withholding tax at a rate that appears relatively reasonable (the US withholding tax rate is 30%) but is really very high when the associated cost of earning the royalty or fee is considered.*

Both the overall and per-country computations would allow the averaging of the various types of foreign taxes incurred on the various types of income. The per-country computation, representing a smaller basket in which to average, would not be as advantageous to the taxpayer as the overall computation. Separate computational baskets for the different types of income would be

---

* Say services were rendered at a 100% mark-up and a $100 fee was earned subject to a 30% foreign withholding tax on the gross amount ($100) paid. The foreign tax would amount to $30 (100 x 0.30 = 30), but the net profit would have been only $50 (100 - 50cost = 50). The foreign rate of tax effectively incurred would be 60% (30 ÷ 50 = 0.60).

Depending on the cost incurred, the effective foreign tax rate could exceed 100% -- for example if the mark-up were only 20% instead of 100%, the effective rate of tax would be 150% (30 ÷ 20 = 1.50).

advantageous to the US Treasury, more so under a per-country computation.

Separate computations for each type of income from each foreign country would best protect the revenues of the US Treasury, but would seem to be burdensome. Its desirability from a tax policy viewpoint would depend on how much of this type of tax gaming takes place.

However dumping the overall computation in favor of a per-country computation would clearly be good tax policy. The overall computation only enhances the US tax incentive to move operations offshore. Both the loophole and the overall computation need to be eliminated because each, in its own way, diminishes US tax revenues, contributes to budget deficits, hurts the US economy and results in the loss of US jobs. This is discussed in the next two chapters, "*Combating Offshore Plundering -- Closing the Foreign Subsidiary Loophole*" and "*Combating Offshore Plundering -- Other Suggested Legislative Changes*."

Chapter 9

Combating Offshore Plundering -- Closing the Foreign Subsidiary Loophole

The foreign subsidiary loophole accounts for the huge offshore cash accumulations maintained by US companies, which accumulations indicate the magnitude of tax avoidance taking place. Using the 2011 estimate of the accumulated offshore cash being $1.375 trillion ($1,375,000,000,000), the tax due the US Treasury would be $385 billion ($385,000,000,000) assuming the foreign tax-rate averaged 10% as suggested in the chapter "*Accumulate Offshore Cash.*"

This would represent the deferred taxes owed the US Treasury and found on the balance sheets of US parent companies, and not include the additional taxes that weren't recorded on the balance sheets because of the permanently reinvested exception.

This book advocates the closing of the loophole and the immediate collection of the deferred taxes and the additional taxes.

The cash is available; it can be taken from the accumulated offshore cash. As the deferred taxes of $385 billion have already been charged to reported earnings when these companies included the foreign income in their financial statements, there will be no charge to reported earnings upon the payment of the deferred taxes. As was indicated in the chapter "*Shareholder Accounting for Offshore Operations (GAAP)*," the additional taxes due because of the permanently invested exception are not so easily estimated, and as to that there will be a charge to earnings upon the closing of the foreign subsidiary loophole.

The cash received by the US Treasury will either balance the Federal budget in the year received or go a long way to that end, or the cash could be used to repay outstanding Federal debt.

Closing the loophole will eliminate the tax incentive to US companies to conduct operations abroad. With the tax incentive purged, the continuing export of US jobs should stop. The process of moving operations and jobs back to United States would begin. The growth of US jobs would enhance domestic purchasing power, improving local markets. Manufacturing capacity in the United States would be rebuilt and the US economic base will broaden. Media and public criticism would lessen as the companies could once again be recognized as being good corporate citizens.

While some US parent companies with offshore cash could benefit from the change in law and advocate the change in law, most US parent companies will be opposed. Most American companies don't benefit at all from the loophole and have been called upon to make up the revenue shortfall created by the loophole, and yet their trade organizations will likely represent the relatively few who do benefit and oppose the loophole plugging.

Some of the companies seeking to preserve the loophole go much further by advocating a repatriation tax holiday that would allow them to bring their accumulated offshore cash home to the United States without the payment of the deferred taxes owe the US Treasury. They say this will allow them to create jobs in the

United States, just as they said in 2005 when they previously got a repatriation tax holiday. Under that tax holiday, they repatriated $312 billion in cash but didn't provide the promised US jobs, using 92% of the cash to pay shareholder dividends and buy-back company stock.

Some companies have the temerity to go even further, advocating that United States adopt the territorial system of taxation where the US only taxes income earned within the United States. This would greatly increase the incentive to move more operations, profits and jobs offshore.

The elimination of the loophole, as argued for in this book, would create US tax neutrality between domestic and foreign operations. Tax neutrality creates a level tax playing-field, allows economics rather than taxes to control.

Some advocates for the elimination of the loophole would probably go further and argue that Congress should penalize American companies who operate abroad and thus force the return of jobs to the United States. While domestic incentives for domestic job would be acceptable, the deliberate retribution against offshore would seem to be inappropriate and violate tax-neutrality.

This book does not advocate the adoption of laws that would penalize offshore operations. This book advocates the elimination of the existing tax incentives for conducting operations offshore so as to create a level playing field. With a level playing field, we could reasonably expect curtailment of job outflow, return of some jobs, and rebuilding the domestic industrial base.

PAYING YOUR "FAIR SHARE" OF TAX is merely empty argumentation as to who should pay more tax or pay less tax. The "fair share" exists only in the eye of the beholder. By the lack of any standard to judge what is fair, the "fair share" comes down to what Congress mandates.

Obviously, our government needs money to run on. Whatever Congress decides to spend money on must ultimately be funded by taxes collected. Borrowing the needed funds can only go so far. Sooner or later the budget has to be balanced and debt paid. So the argument as to who should pay more or less tax goes on and on, from one Congress to the next, and will continue forever.

However, there is one thing we all can and should agree to. While we might believe that the presently mandated tax-rates are either to too high or too low, or believe that the tax system is skewed in one fashion or another, we can all agree that mandated taxes should be paid.

Closing loopholes and blocking unintended consequences would certainly be part of everybody's striving for fairness. The questions faced are whether the loopholes exist or not, and whether unintended consequences have gone too far. If so, the loopholes should be plugged and intended outcomes restored.

Others are being forced to pay higher taxes to make up for the lost tax collections. When the tax burden is so shifted, the companies and individuals who have to pay more would, by definition, be paying more than their fair share.

It is not a question of live-and-let-live. Those who cheat, or take advantage of tax loopholes or game the tax laws do impact others. While arguing about paying a "fair share" leads nowhere, closing loopholes and countering tax cheats and tax gamers does make the tax system fairer.

WHEN TAX GAMING HAS GONE TOO FAR, those of us who pay the tax price for it have an obligation to speak out. Congress has responded in the recent past. A situation similar to the one we now face occurred back in in the 1980s.

At that time, financial engineering ran rampart with all sorts of tax shelters for individuals. The rich were bombarded with schemes to avoid or evade tax by investing in tax shelters, many of which were very dubious or criminally illegal. It got to the point where tax sheltering got down to the man in the street, no longer being just for the rich.

Taxpayers were induced to invest in real estate so that the depreciation deductions would offset professional income or wages and little or no tax would have to be paid. That was the most popular tax shelter. These real estate tax shelters were legitimate, allowed by the tax laws enacted by Congress.

Other tax shelters weren't legitimate, but at first the IRS didn't have the expertness to even identify them. The financial engineers ran circles around the IRS. Also, the IRS didn't have sufficient staff to enforce the tax laws.

Some legislators were so opposed to taxation that they resorted to taking it out on IRS funding. By starving the IRS, they effectively showed that they were willing to condone cheating. The IRS was ineffective against the dubious and illegal tax shelters.

Real estate tax shelters couldn't be attacked by the IRS, even if it had the staff to do so, because they were legitimate. And those tax shelters had a handy and appealing justification argument; that the country needed the additional investments in real estate.

The matter came to a head in the 1980s when it became apparent that any taxpayer could, and too many did, shelter their income (professional fees, wages, royalties, services income, whatever) from tax. The US tax base was sorely eroding.

Congress acted to change the unintended consequences of the tax laws Congress previously mandated as being best for the country. Congress set up a shield around all forms of earned income (fees, wages, royalties, etc.) so that passive losses from tax shelter investments couldn't offset the taxes the US Treasury would normally collect on the earned income. That preserved the earned income tax base.

Needless to say, the financial engineers didn't like this and many taxpayers who took advantage of the situation objected, arguing that the change was unfair. Congress rightfully put such arguments aside and changed the law even though the change was unpopular in many quarters. After all, nobody likes to pay tax. Congress had to act in order to preserve the US tax base, as it does now in order to preserve the corporate tax base.

We currently find a similar situation created by the ever increasing offshore operations of US parent companies. The US corporate tax base is being eroded. On each budget go-around, Congress is finding it harder and harder to raise taxes to fund the government. The argument faced is that taxes are high enough, so the curtailment of vital services is pursued while the culprit is the avoidance of huge amounts of US tax through the use of the foreign subsidiary loophole in our worldwide taxation system.

President Ronald Reagan also spoke about things getting "far out of line" when he closed corporate loopholes in the 1980s.*

THE BUDGETARY EFFECT of eliminating the loophole and immediately collecting the deferred taxes owned the US Treasury is not known but could be estimated by economists or researchers. In the initial year, the catch-up tax collection of the previously deferred taxes might possibly balance the budget and put it into a surplus. That would be a one-time event.

As the existing offshore cash hoards do seem to be "extra" cash not used or needed in the business, there should be enough cash available to pay the deferred taxes. As there will be no charge to reported earnings upon the payment of the deferred tax, wailing against paying that liability should fail to deter immediate collection.

---

* "*G.E.'s Strategies Let It Avoid Taxes Altogether*," by David Kocieniewski, The New York Times, March 24, 2011.

In addition to the deferred taxes that appear on the books of account, there is a possibility that much more tax is owed on the offshore earning of foreign subsidiaries on which no deferred tax had been provided on the books because of the permanent reinvestment exception discussed earlier. Special care should be taken in drafting the language closing of the foreign subsidiary loophole to assure the collection of such taxes.

While the managements of US parent companies that did not use this exemption might go along with, or even favor, the elimination of the foreign subsidiary loophole because there would be no charge to earnings for them, those who used the exemption could be expected to strongly oppose the closing of the foreign subsidiary loophole or pursue an exception for their exception.

Estimates of the potential amount at stake in this might be gleaned from the tax footnotes in the detailed SEC filings of US parent companies, but the disclosure requirements are not clear.

THE US ECONOMIC BASE has been eroding. In previous decades, in the good old days, the United States grew mightily. Now we have more and deeper recessions. We still have the largest economy in the world, but relatively speaking we are falling behind while other countries are moving ahead rapidly.

Our companies developed wonderful new products, recently the iProducts, but the rest of the world seems to benefit from it more than we do. Those products are manufactured offshore, providing jobs to foreign workers and growing their economic base.* All we have to show for our ingenuity is some giant US companies with growing profits that don't add to the domestic economic base. Those profits are the second prize or third prize, the first prize is going offshore.

---

* "*How the U.S. Lost Out on iPhone Work*," by Charles Duhigg and Keith Bradsher, The New York Times, January 21, 2012

This is also shown in the relative well-being of the people, here and abroad. The standard of living abroad is growing in double-digits while the standard of living domestically stagnates. Our economy is growing very slowly and our people are not doing very well,* with the reverse taking place abroad. We had the ingenuity and know-how here to develop the new iProducts, and we'll surely develop the next generation of products, but all we'll have to show for it because of the foreign subsidiary loophole is additional financial profits. Everything else goes offshore.

This is a cutting edge. We have the financial profits but the economic base is shifting abroad. We have to change what we do, and eliminating the foreign subsidiary loophole which provides a US tax incentive to conduct operations abroad should be at the top of the list. Some companies are beginning to see the light,† but that should not deter or delay Congress in closing the loophole.

MORE US JOBS will materialize when the foreign subsidiary loophole is closed. The shifting of existing US jobs will then moderate or cease. Some US jobs will still be lost to lower wages abroad, but that too will moderate as foreign wages increase and foreign societies change‡ as they appear to be doing. However, rising wages in one foreign country frequently leads to shifting operations to another foreign country with lower wages.

With the elimination of the foreign subsidiary loophole, the return of some jobs to the United States should be expected. As the foreign subsidiary loophole also provided an incentive to expand foreign plants instead of US plants, the elimination of the

---

* "*Our Economic Pickle*," by Steven Greenhouse, The New York Times, January 12, 2013.

† "*Walmart Plans to Buy American More Often*," by Stephanie Clifford, The New York Times, January 15, 2013.

‡ "*Chinese Graduates Say No Thanks to Factory Jobs*," By Keith Bradsher, The New York Times, January 24, 2013.

loophole will create a more level playing field and lead to more domestic plant expansions.

As the recent recession has shown, it had become more difficult to create US jobs during the economic recovery than it had been after previous recessions. Thus, creating US jobs though the plugging the foreign subsidiary loophole becomes especially attractive if not imperative.

Arguing for the Status Quo

It is difficult to argue in favor of continuing the foreign subsidiary loophole. The arguments being made are not supported in fact or are specious. The argument could be for consistency, for preserving the separate status of foreign subsidiaries, for not being put at a disadvantage to foreign rivals, and for needing the foreign subsidiary loophole so as to allow of businesses to escape overregulation in the United States.

There are also arguments that are not aimed at preserving the status quo but seek to do better than the status quo by reducing corporate taxes even more. These arguments would include the most basic one of eliminating "double taxation" by going to a territorial taxation system, of having a repatriation tax holiday, of reducing the US corporate tax-rate, or of adopting a minimum tax on offshore earnings.

THE CONSISTENCY ARGUMENT is that fairness requires that laws not be changed after those laws have been relied on. Yet, everybody knows that all laws can and have been changed from time to time, and that not even the Constitution is carved in stone. The consistency argument is essentially that there should never be any changes to what was previously done.

We know that is baseless as there as there has never been consistency in our tax laws or in any other laws. It has been rightfully said time and time again that one Congress cannot bind another Congress.

Yet those who advance the consistency argument are themselves inconsistent in arguing for tax-rate reduction, repatriation tax holidays and other things they favor. Like extoling a steady and true course, the consistency argument is mere rhetoric

THE SEPARATE STATUS OF A FOREIGN SUBSIDIARY is not undermined by including it the US consolidated tax return of the US parent company, just like domestic subsidiaries are included. Both domestic and foreign subsidiaries are included in a parent company's consolidated financial statements. Separate corporate status is not destroyed or even altered by the inclusion of foreign subsidiary financial results in parent company reporting for accounting or tax purposes.

The foreign subsidiary would not become subject to US tax by including their earning in the US parent company tax return; their earnings are included so as to determine the tax owed by, and to be paid by, the US parent company. No tax is levied on the foreign subsidiary.

The primary purpose of incorporating the foreign subsidiary remains fulfilled, whether it was to insulate the parent from the liabilities of the subsidiary or whether practicalities required use of a separate corporate entity.

The independence of a subsidiary continues to be recognized even though such independence is fictional because the subsidiary is invariably the alter-ego of its parent company. While this independent status might be challenged as a matter of equity by someone swindled under the corporate veil, the separate status of a subsidiary is established law and not generally challenged. The inclusion of a foreign subsidiary in the US parent company's tax return does not deny the subsidiary's existence as an entity nor its independent status.

BEING PUT AT A DISADVANTAGE TO FOREIGN RIVALS is the basic argument made by US companies opposed to the elimination of the foreign subsidiary loophole. They are essentially arguing for a lower US corporate tax rate as their technically competent rivals are subject to tax-rates hovering around 25% except for Japan where the rate is somewhat higher than the US corporate tax rate of 35%. Their argument is fallacious in a number of respects.

It is rare indeed when a higher tax-rate deters a successful company from operating in a country. Many foreign rivals have not hesitated to commence operations in the United States because they would be subject to a higher tax-rate here than they encounter at home. And there is no way to quantify the value to a US company of being from the United States with US influence, power and cachet behind it, all paid for by the higher US tax-rate.

There is a 10% differential in tax-rates between the approximate 25% tax-rate* the foreign rivals are subject to and the 35% US tax rate. If this 10% differential truly impacted the ability of American corporations to compete abroad, the American

---

* China has a 25% tax-rate and offers a lower 15% tax-rate to attract industries encouraged by the Chinese government (primarily new tech and high tech enterprises and certain integrated circuits production enterprises). The Chinese tax system operates in a competitive fashion to attract the industries it wants to attract while the US tax system operates to drive US companies offshore.
Korea has a tax rate of 22% plus a 10% surcharge, making for a 24% tax rate, and has a worldwide taxation system very similar to that of the United States. Japan recently reduced its statutory tax-rate from 30% to 25.5% but adds a host of other taxes that brings the overall rate to above 35%.
OECD counties average about a 26% corporate tax-rate, higher in the more technically advanced countries.

corporations wouldn't have been as successful as they have been offshore.

Nor can it rationally be argued that it is the non-payment of the US tax by virtue of the foreign subsidiary loophole that allows American companies to successfully compete against their foreign rivals.

The salient fact remains that American companies have enviable profits abroad and are very successful in competing against foreign rival with the US tax-rate being where it is. So where is the complaint? The complaint is that these companies want lower tax-rates -- we all do. But to say that American companies are losing out to their foreign rivals is false.

OVERREGULATION IN THE UNITED STATES is sometimes cited as justification for US corporations to go offshore. Regulation versus overregulation might, like beauty, be in the eye of the beholder. But even if the United States can be said to overregulate, that would be no justification for the United States to provide a tax incentive for US companies to go offshore. If there is overregulation in the United States, going offshore to avoid that overregulation might be reason enough if the overregulation is as terrible as it is said to be; it need not be bolstered by a US tax incentive to go offshore.

Nevertheless, there is no overregulation in the United States. The facts show that overregulation in the United States is not amongst the reasons US companies go offshore. The World Bank rated the United States as being the 4th easiest in which to operate a business.* Mainland China was rated 91st in the list and yet US companies are flocking to conduct business there.

---

* "*Is Overregulation Driving U.S. Companies Offshore?*" by Catherine Rampell, The New York Times, November 7, 2011.

Whatever the reason for going offshore in China, it obviously isn't as a reaction to overregulation in the United States.

ELIMINATING "DOUBLE TAXATION" is attractive rhetoric for it sounds like the taxes are being imposed twice, creating an unfair double burden.

As has been pointed out in some detail, our tax system employs a foreign tax credit mechanism that eliminates double taxation. Opponents use "double taxation" as slogan whereas our taxing system only brings the overall tax to the US tax-rate, creating tax neutrality between domestic and offshore operations which are thereby taxed as the same rate.

The elimination of the foreign subsidiary loophole serves the same purpose by eliminating the loophole advantage for foreign operation and again fostering tax neutrality. Tax neutrality is surely where we should want to be.

In labeling our current tax system as "double taxation," those who favor the foreign subsidiary loophole are effectively arguing for a territorial system of taxation. They want to eliminate any US tax on foreign income, which is territorial taxation. A territorial tax system would certainly fill-up the ships going abroad with US jobs and totally destroy the US economic base.

IMPOSING A MINIMUM TAX ON OFFSHORE EARNINGS has been given some thought as a way to encourage business investment in the United States. The minimum tax could be structured to tax all foreign income immediately (which would eliminate the foreign subsidiary loophole), and tax the foreign income at either a higher or lower of tax than is applicable to domestic income.

If the foreign income is to be taxed at a higher rate than domestic income, it would be a deliberate penalty on foreign operations and violate tax neutrality. This should be opposed.

If the foreign income is to be taxed as a lower rate than domestic income, it would still leave an incentive to operate offshore; perhaps a greater incentive than the foreign subsidiary loophole presently provides depending on the tax-rate specified. This too violates tax neutrality and should be opposed.

A REPATRIATION TAX HOLIDAY is once again being pursued, perhaps because the US parent companies believe that their accumulated cash balances have gotten to intolerable levels. More likely, it is just to get another handout like they got in 2005.

The first repatriation tax holiday was ill-advised for many reasons, including that it would create an even stronger incentive to continue accumulating cash abroad until another repatriation tax holiday could be obtained. And so it did.

The new repatriation tax holiday isn't being pursued because the experience with the last one was good (it wasn't) but just to obtain another handout; another undeserved windfall profit. One would have thought that this ploy for a handout would be dead.

The last experience was awful because the backers of the tax holiday promised to invest the repatriated cash to create US jobs, a promise not kept* since almost all of the repatriated cash went to pay shareholder dividends and buy back company stock. It became painfully obvious that there was no desire to invest money in the United State because any opportunity presented domestically

---

* One company claimed having increased domestic R&D expenditures, increased US capital expenditures and increased US salaries and wage while regulatory filings showed it cut back its work force and capital expenditures. "*Companies Push for Tax Break on Foreign Cash*," by David Kocieniewski, The New York Times, June 19, 2011.

could be pursued offshore and, in so doing, take even more advantage of the foreign subsidiary loophole.

This is the rub. The US companies that have taken so much advantage of the foreign subsidiary loophole so as to have built up those huge offshore cash accumulations would stick to their mindset and continue to pursue foreign investments rather purse domestic investment. Their mindset effectively blinds them to US business opportunities. With the previous experience, the repatriation tax holiday should be dead. No assurance of domestic jobs or other benefits should be accepted because of what previously happened.

Keep in mind that the companies pursuing the repatriation tax holiday are giant companies as shown by their having brought back over $300 billion[*] in offshore cash the last time. Their new promises should not be accepted for still other reasons. These giant companies have the wherewithal to pursue whatever they are promising without a tax holiday by merely using the extensive domestic resources they surely have. Also, they could repatriate and pay the tax if domestic investment is truly attractive to them.

The repatriation tax holiday is to be distinguished from the exception for active financing. The active financing exception allows foreign subsidiaries in the financing business to indirectly bring offshore cash back to the United States in order to finance US exports,[†] a seemingly worthwhile endeavor except that the offshore cash was created by the foreign subsidiary loophole.

Without getting into the merits or demerits of the active financing exception (or why domestic funds couldn't be used, or why the offshore cash couldn't be repatriated and the deferred US tax paid), it differs from a repatriation tax holiday which is a

[*] "*Bringing Cash Back to U.S. With Reduced Taxes*," by Jesse Drucker, The New York Times, Bloomberg News, December 29, 2010, also appearing in The International Herald Tribune on December 30, 2010.

[†] "*G.E.'s Strategies Let It Avoid Taxes Altogether*," by David Kocieniewski , The New York Times, March 24, 2011.

permanent handout. Under the active financing exception, the eventually cash returns to offshore coffers and, presumably, deferred taxes are provided on the profits earned in the foreign subsidiaries.

Nevertheless, closing the foreign subsidiary loophole will eliminate the cry for repatriation tax holidays and also eliminate the active financing exception for then the offshore cash could either be left for use abroad or brought back to the United States as there would be tax-neutrality between offshore and domestic financing.

LOWERING THE US CORPORATE TAX-RATE can be cast as being an inducement to bring the huge offshore cash hoards back to the United States, and thereby lessen the value of eliminating the foreign subsidiary loophole. However, this would preserve the incentive to move operations abroad as the deferral tax benefit would still exist. A somewhat lower tax-rate would do little to bring the accumulated offshore cash home, but it would yield pleasant tax reduction and also a windfall profit.

The reduction of the US corporate tax-rate is presently being advocated in Washington, but coupled with the elimination of loopholes and other changes that would make for revenue neutrality. That is, there would be no overall reduction in corporate taxes, but just changes in how the same amount of tax revenues would be obtained from the same group; it just shuffles tax around within the corporate group. Whether particular corporations would favor such an approach would depend on where the changes fall. Every corporation can be expected to fight for the preservation of any existing tax provision favoring them or fight for a quid pro quo in yielding it.

Loopholes should be closed anyway, not be made part of any deal, because the loopholes were unintended. Loopholes never came into the law because of any thought-through deal and shouldn't become part of any negotiated deal when they are eliminated. A good case can be made for closing the foreign subsidiary loophole and keeping that closing out of any revenue-neutral deal or any tax-rate discussion.

But should the foreign subsidiary loophole be closed in some sort of a deal, the deal should not include forgiving taxes already owed. The deferred taxes due the US Treasury should be collected as a debt owed, along with collecting the tax owed on other offshore income on which deferred tax had not been provided. Tax-reduction or tax-reshuffling deals are prospective, and existing tax liabilities should be paid just like any other liability should be paid. Forgiveness of a liability would be an unjustifiable handout, a windfall, and that is the way the accountants would show it on the financial statements..

Reduction in the US corporate tax-rate going beyond revenue-neutrality (that is, real tax-rate reduction resulting in lower US Treasury revenues) presents different political considerations. We do not need to reduce our tax revenues in order to help American corporations compete against their foreign rivals; they have competed very well under the old tax rates.

A much better use of the tax revenues that would be lost in really reducing the US tax-rate would be in helping American companies develop new products by giving grants for the development of new technology and the like. That this is the way to go is shown by a domestic company that got $249 million in grants from the US government and failed still having value and winding up being purchased in a bidding contest after the company went bankrupt.* The grants are the cutting edge, not tax-rates.

Tax-rate reduction would accomplish little. Even an unjustifiably large tax-rate reduction would not induce the tax

---

* "*Chinese Firm Wins Bid for Auto Battery Maker*," by Bill Vlasic, The New York Times, December 9, 2012.

cheats to stop cheating. Moderately lower tax-rates do not reduce the incentive to game taxes or to pursue new loopholes.

The incentive to conduct business and earn profits, as much profit as possible, will remain whether the corporate tax-rate is a little higher or lower. Perversely, one could argue that a higher tax-rate would induce harder work so as to meet earnings goals. Of course, this is nonsense as are the other fringe arguments.

All the peripheral arguments for a lower or higher tax-rate should be disregarded as the corporate tax-rate decision is and should remain a political decision based on where Congress wants to get the money from to run the government.

Nevertheless, if a lower US corporate tax-rate were to be enacted before the already outstanding deferred taxes owed to the US Treasury had to be paid, the amount owed would be at the new lower tax-rate and result in a windfall profit to the US parent companies owing the tax. This would be a free-ride and should be avoided, the foreign subsidiary loophole closed and the deferred taxes collected at the present tax-rate.

Chapter 10

Combating Offshore Plundering -- Other Suggested Legislative Changes

While the elimination of the foreign subsidiary loophole is the most important tax change Congress can enact, there are a few other legislative changes that could and should be made while Congress's attention is focused on international taxation.

Adopt a Per-Country Foreign Tax Credit

Our overall foreign tax credit limitation should be replaced by a per-country foreign tax credit limitation under which the income from each foreign country is treated separately.

The credit for foreign taxes is limited to the US tax-rate. The per-country computation does not allow a credit for foreign taxes in excess of the US tax rate. The overall computation allows for a credit for foreign taxes that exceed the US tax-rate because of the way averaging works. This has been fully explained in the chapter "*Avoiding Double Taxation -- The US Foreign Tax Credit System.*"

The overall computation should be abandoned legislatively in favor of the per-country limitation because it runs afoul of the basic proposition that the United States should not bear the burden of foreign taxes in excess of the US tax-rate, and it is the taxpayer that chooses to subject itself to paying the higher taxes.

On the more practical level, in addition to the overall computation allowing a US parent company to saddle the US Treasury with the higher tax the company incurs in the normal course of business, the company could deliberately negotiate paying a higher tax in exchange for some special advantage from the foreign government -- the US Treasury bears the burden of the higher tax under the overall limitation while the company benefits from the special advantage. In a version of this, the overall credit also allows a foreign government to negotiate a higher tax-rate with those in a specific industry for giving the industry what it wants.

There is no theoretical justification for the overall computation and every practical reason to do away with it.

SEPARATE COMPUTATIONS FOR DIFFERENT TYPES OF INCOME earned in each country could be mandated under the per-country computation approach. Combining the various types of income (e.g., business earnings and royalty income) that can arise in a country would allow averaging of the different tax-rates the foreign country could have on these types of income. Again, the financial engineer can game the situation. For instance, instead of paying a fee or price for something the foreign government supplies, a royalty subject to a high tax-rate could be structured so that the tax gets passed onto the US Treasury through the averaging within the per-country foreign tax credit.

While separate type-of-income computations for each country would be an added taxpayer clerical burden, it wouldn't be much of a problem in this digital age. However, it is not known how widespread this type of gamesmanship might be and whether the separate type-of-income computations are worth mandating.

Nevertheless, mandating a separate per-county computation for the income arising in each country is clearly warranted if not imperative.

Adopt Legislation to See-Through Sham Entities

Deceptive business structures are the relatively recent invention of financial engineers. A special purpose vehicle, frequently in the form of a partnership, is formed that nobody seems to own. It is not a matter of foreign bank secrecy or corporate registrar secrecy. The structure of the vehicle itself is at issue.

The public accountants have to determine whether their client, a US parent company, has to include (consolidate) the vehicle in the client's shareholder financial statements.* Frequently the accountants rely on legal opinions as to basic matters but the consolidation decision rests with the accountants.

Dubious or sham vehicles are used for "off balance sheet financing." The issue is whether the client was using the vehicle in order to hide a borrowing (that is, hide a loan really to it or to one

---

* "*Deals That Helped Doom Enron Began to Form in the Early 90's*," by Kurt Eichenwald with Michael Brick, The New York Times, January 18, 2002.

of its subsidiaries by an outside party) that should appear on its balance sheet. If that were the case, the client would normally have been involved in the formation of the vehicle and there would be some connections between the client or its subsidiaries and the vehicle.

If the vehicle was found to be owned by the client, it would have to be treated as a subsidiary of the client and included in its financial statements, thereby converting what was designed to be off balance sheet financing into on balance sheet financing. Off balance sheet financing is predicated on not owning the vehicle. If you don't own it, you can't consolidate it.

Some in the accounting profession accept the existence of off balance-sheet financing, which appears to be a misnomer inasmuch as nothing a company does should theoretically be off its balance-sheet. All company assets, liabilities and activities should be reflected on a company's books of account. Yet off balance-sheet borrowings had incomprehensibly been accepted by some in the accounting profession, invariably backed up by written legal opinions. Leases, sometimes a substitute for borrowings, are different as they have to be disclosed and readers of the financial statements could view the lease payments owed as borrowing if they wish to.

Legislatively combating the sham vehicles would be difficult as the matter of definition would be very challenging. However, a rebuttable presumption could be legislated based on some of the common features pointing in an evident direction as to ownership. For instance, looking to who was involved during the formation process, who dealt with the vehicle, and who wound up with the money could be the key indicia in designing the presumption.

The existence of such a presumption, imperfect as it would surely be, should make it uncomfortable for the accountants to accept the legal opinions and for the lawyers to write them. More important, the uncertainty created by such a presumption should dissuade management from going forward with that kind of endeavor.

Dump Withholding Exemption Certificates and Start the Actual Withholding of Tax

Tax cheating on the international level, where money moves around the world so as to escape tax, has grown to such an extent that the tax authorities can no longer effectively enforce the tax laws.* Back in 2002 it was estimated that offshore tax evasion cost the US Treasury $70 billion annually,† not a sum that honest taxpayers gladly pay to make up the revenue shortfall. It didn't get any better ten years later.‡

The offshore money invariably winds up in locations that allow the owners to escape tax in their home countries and in the countries where the funds are invested.

Perhaps we should only be concerned with Americans, individuals and corporations, participating in this. But drug cartel money, terrorist money and other money also benefit from these tax evasion practices. And money that escapes taxation compounds faster, providing a significant long-term advantage in terms of their growth as well as the growth and economic power of the countries they reside in.

Money invested in the United States by a foreign person produces income sourced in the United States which could be taxed here; the United States has a right to tax all income earned

---

* "*Tax Enforcer Says Cheating Is on the Rise*," by David Cay Johnston, The New York Times, July 19, 2001.

† "*Departing Chief Says I.R.S. Is Losing Its War on Tax Cheats*," by David Cay Johnson, The New York Times, November 5, 2002.

‡ "*These Islands Aren't Just a Shelter From Taxes*," by David Cay Johnston, The New York Times, May 5, 2012.

here. It would be the primary right to tax as we have seen the foreign person's country giving a credit for the US tax, unless the primary right to tax is relinquished by tax treaty. Most of the industrial developed nations have similar withholding tax systems.

The existing systems and practices might have worked many decades ago when they were set up. They still sound good in theory but in practice they just don't work. Now there are multitudes of statutory and tax treaty exceptions and exemptions that are used as loopholes, and now there are also more extensive and complex exemption certificate procedures that allow for wholesale tax avoidance around the world. There is a way to clean up a good part of this, but first a little quirk about money must be understood.

Money produces income (think interest) where it is put to work. It is put to work in places like the United States and other developed and even less-developed countries where there are investment opportunities. When funds are transferred to a tax-haven rock in the middle of the ocean where hardly any business is conducted locally, it should be obvious that the funds must flow off the rock to be placed in actual use. In one fashion or another that money goes to the countries were it could find use.

Thus, if the United States and the other countries would actually withhold their withholding taxes (the US rate is 30%) on all payments to foreign persons, the money flowing to the tax-haven rocks would have been subject to tax and the tax cheats, drug cartels, terrorists and the others who bank there would have to bear the financial burden. To be sure, some money could have gone to other places where there are lower or no taxes, but not much and at greater risk and probably lower yields.

This necessitates dumping the existing exemption certificate and other procedures that allow cross-border flows without actual withholding. It would also require and allow tightening up of the many statutory exemptions to withholding. Across-the-board withholding in this digital age would be much more efficient than the many hoops payers and recipients have to go through. Today there are all sorts of paper filing requirements for beneficial holders, non-beneficial holders, partnerships, trusts and other types of vehicles, even so-called "flow-through" entities. And the payers of the income have to deal with this morass of payer and build systems to deal with all the exceptions and special cases.

It also appears that the exemption certificate procedure can be abused in reputable and reliable venues like the United Kingdom, a favorite of the financial engineers. The US-UK tax treaty provides an exemption from withholding taxes for parties who prove they are entitled to the benefits of the treaty, but the financial engineers seem to get around that and flow money in and out of the United Kingdom without tax irrespective of who the parties are.

So the proposition is simple while the execution will take time and be difficult. Concisely put, there should be actual withholding of tax on cross-border flows except only where it makes no absolutely sense (like in government to government flows). Across-the-board withholding would simplify things in this computer age, and periodic inter-government payments can be used to get the withheld money into the right country as determined by tax treaty.

A multi-country agreement to dump the exemptions and adopt actual withholding has to be reached, always a difficult thing* made more difficult by the likely opposition of the tax-haven countries and their banks, financial engineers and others who benefit from the existing practices. But if it can be done, expect some tax-havens and banks to close, expect the tax cheats to come home, expect the tax authorities to get on top of their

---

* "*A Retreat on Tax Havens*," Opinion, The New York Times, May 26, 2001. "*Backing Sought for Offshore Tax Initiative*," Opinion, The New York Times, June 14, 2001. "*Tax Haven Crackdown Creates Opportunities for Bankers,*" by Mark Scott, The New York Times, April 5, 2012.

workloads, and expect government revenues around the world to blossom.

The author of this book made a similar suggestion[*] in a professional tax magazine almost two decades ago; to absolutely no avail. Perhaps, its time has come.

---

* "*Why Don't We Tax Foreigners Like We Tax Ourselves? Financial Competitiveness,*" TAX NOTES. Page 875, Vol 66, No 6, February 6, 1995.

Made in the USA
Monee, IL
04 November 2026

67378947R00066